P9-CMT-145

The Enemy Has a Face

The Enemy Has a Face
The Seeds of Peace Experience

John Wallach

with Michael Wallach

Photographs by James Lukoski

UNITED STATES INSTITUTE OF PEACE PRESS

Washington, D.C.

The views expressed in this book are those of the author alone. They do not necessarily reflect views of the United States Institute of Peace.

United States Institute of Peace
1200 17th Street NW
Washington, DC 20036

© 2000 by the Endowment of the United States Institute of Peace. All photographs copyright James Lukoski 1999. All rights reserved.

First published 2000

Printed in the United States of America

The paper used in this publication meets the minimum requirements of American National Standards for Information Sciences—Permanence of Paper for Printed Library Materials, ANSI Z39.48-1984.

Library of Congress Cataloging-in-Publication Data
Wallach, John.
    The enemy has a face : the Seeds of Peace experience / John Wallach with Michael Wallach.
      p. cm.
    ISBN 1-878379-97-6 (cloth : alk. paper) — ISBN 1-878379-96-8 (paper : alk. paper)
    1. Arab-Israeli confilct—1993– 2. Teenagers, Palestinian Arab—Middle East—Attitudes. 3. Jewish teenagers—Israel—Attitudes. 4. Teenagers and peace. 5. Group relations training—Maine. 6. Social interaction in adolescence—Maine. 7. Seeds of Peace Program. I. Wallach, Michael. II. Title.

    DS119.76.W35 2000
    303.6'6—dc21   99-044993

to Janet,
my facilitator,
with love

CONTENTS

FOREWORD

Generations of Israelis and Palestinians have been taught to hate and fear each other. In the Middle East—as in the former Yugoslavia, on the island of Cyprus, and in so many other places around the world where ethnic and religious antagonisms keep communities in confrontation—young people are routinely exposed to education in hatred. For decades, even centuries, such hostility has fueled national conflicts, communal massacres, and the systematic expulsions that the world knows of today by the chilling term "ethnic cleansing." Can this pattern be broken? Can communities burdened with mutual distrust and the desire to avenge past wrongs escape from the cycle of self-destructive conflict?

John Wallach's innovative and inspiring Seeds of Peace program was designed to deal with this fundamental human challenge: How to break the generational cycle of hostility that perpetuates confrontations and fuels outbreaks of violence?

Seeds of Peace was established in 1993 to give Arab and Israeli young-sters the opportunity to look at the world afresh, to rise above the hatreds of their elders, and to develop a shared desire to create a new world free of hostility and violence. That, to be sure, is a bold ambition, but in only six brief years the Seeds of Peace program has achieved remarkable results. Almost everyone who learns about this program finds Seeds of Peace inspir-ing. Even hardened politicians, skeptical diplomats, and world-weary jour-nalists find themselves sensing a more hopeful future when they hear what the young people in the program—the "seeds of peace"—are up to.

Why? In part, it's the obvious emotional appeal of the idea of hundreds of youngsters from very different backgrounds living, playing, and working together for three weeks in the beautiful woods of Maine. In part, it is the realization that these teenagers aren't just from different backgrounds but from opposite sides of one of the world's bloodiest and longest-running conflicts, the Arab-Israeli confrontation. When, as so often happens, the prospects for finding a peaceful solution to that conflict fade amid the gloom of new violence and renewed assertions of old hatreds, Seeds of Peace stands as one of the few beacons of hope still shining in the Middle East.

That said, perhaps the single most inspiring thing about Seeds of Peace is not what the program does, or may do, in the Middle East, but rather how the program actually works. At its heart—or so it seems to me after reading this book—Seeds of Peace works by dispelling ignorance, destroying stereotypes, dissipating hatred—and building human relationships. This is an encouraging finding in its own context, but it also suggests that what John Wallach and his colleagues have learned about the process of reconciling Arab and Israeli youngsters can be applied to other conflicts. In short, the Seeds of Peace methodology, I believe, has universal relevance.

John Wallach, Barbara Gottschalk, Tim Wilson, and the talented counselors, facilitators, artists, and other staff who help run the program in Maine don't try to indoctrinate the teenagers in one or another argument about what caused the Arab-Israeli conflict. Nor do they try to persuade the Egyptian, Israeli, Jordanian, Moroccan, Palestinian, Tunisian, Qatari, and Yemeni youngsters about how the conflict can best be resolved. What they try to do, and what they seem to achieve, is to help the campers discover how little they know about their adversaries, about themselves, and about how much they have to gain by building the friendships that are the seeds of a constructive future.

Much of the time spent at camp—whether on the sports fields, in the art and computer rooms, in the sometimes raucous dining hall, or in the daily two-hour "coexistence sessions" where the youngsters argue their positions and vent their anger and frustration—is devoted to exposing ignorance or misinformation and replacing it with mutual understanding and humanized relationships. Typically, the campers arrive in Maine somewhat apprehensive but eager to explain why their own government's cause is just and why the "other side" is wrong. They also arrive weighed down by distrust and prejudice. They think they know what to expect of themselves and of their counterparts from the other side. Gradually, over three short but intensive weeks of common living, they come to discover that many of their preconceptions are wrong and that there is a shared human reality that transcends differences in background.

The simple fact of living with youngsters from the other side does much to dispel prejudice: It is hard to continue to believe that all Palestinians are supporters of political violence or that all Israelis are indifferent to the consequences of the Israeli military occupation when you have gotten to know the Palestinians on your soccer team and the Israelis sitting at your dinner table. More than that, however, the Seeds of Peace program urges each camper to "make one friend" with a camper from among the "enemy." Stereotypes are even harder to maintain when you don't merely play together or sit next to someone in the dining hall, but when you actually learn to like them, share personal secrets, or find common ground. Interaction and mutual understanding are further encouraged in the coexistence sessions, where every day each camper joins eleven other youngsters to exchange opinions and arguments about the issues that divide them.

The camp experience is emotionally and psychologically challenging—indeed, as John has discovered, it *has* to be challenging if the youngsters are to undergo a real and lasting transformation in attitudes. Sometimes a political crisis back home will erupt in the middle of camp that calls upon the youngsters to choose between retreating to the safety of their own side and their old prejudices or making the effort to work through painful issues with new friends. Often the coexistence sessions will reach a point where, with each side having shouted its arguments at the other, the youngsters will suddenly begin to listen—to themselves as well as to the others. As they do so, they discover the pain and the suffering that burdens *both* sides, and they learn that the stereotypes of the enemy they arrived with don't fit anymore. They see that the enemy does in fact have a face, a unique, individual face— a face not so different from their own. Moreover, they discover that their image of themselves also doesn't fit as well as once it did. They may unearth feelings—of blind hatred for the other side, for example—that they would prefer not to have found. They may discover that their opinions about the conflict were actually the opinions of their teachers or families or governments, and that those opinions now seem badly flawed.

Having helped the youngsters confront their own misconceptions of themselves and the "other," the program leaves it to the youngsters to decide what to replace such distortions and ignorance with. In a remarkable number of cases they opt for tolerance and understanding, for deepening friendships and increasing contacts with those who come from the other side of the conflict. They embrace the dream of a peaceful, cooperative relationship with former adversaries, and they return to their home communities determined to turn dream into reality.

But friendships made in the safe haven of rustic New England are vulnerable to disparagement when the campers return to societies that may condemn mere contact with the "enemy." Family and friends re-envelop the youngsters in deeply entrenched attitudes weighted with a society's culture and institutions. To help the campers deal with the scorn and opposition they may encounter, the Seeds of Peace program works to sustain their new sense of community. The program recently opened an office in Jerusalem that helps hundreds of Seeds of Peace graduates keep in touch with one another in a variety of ways. They travel across heavily guarded borders to visit one another's homes and high schools. They organize baseball and soccer games among not only the alumni themselves but also their friends. They write and produce an alumni newspaper, *The Olive Branch*. And they make extensive use of the Seeds of Peace Internet site, constantly exchanging e-mails on subjects both personal and political, sharing opinions and seeking advice and support when they run into hostility from families, friends, teachers, or others still locked into a zero-sum view of the Arab-Israeli confrontation.

The Seeds of Peace program also organizes special events that bring together alumni to negotiate among themselves on the thorny issues that continue to divide their nations and peoples, and to craft appeals to their political leaders to compromise for the sake of peace. In ten or twenty years, these teenage "seeds of peace" will grow to become leaders in their societies, leaders able to fashion or defend a lasting peace directly.

The value of the Seeds of Peace experience lies not only in what it may accomplish within the Middle East, but also in the model it offers for an approach to fostering mutual understanding and reconciliation between other longtime adversaries. To give John Wallach an opportunity to reflect on how his program works and to put his conclusions into writing, the United States Institute of Peace awarded him a Jennings Randolph Senior Fellowship in 1998–99. The result of his "time off" is this book, which we believe will be an illuminating and stimulating resource for a wide range of readers. Written in the engaging, clear-sighted style one would expect of a distinguished journalist, *The Enemy Has a Face* is an excellent introduction to the human dimension of the Arab-Israeli conflict and to a process of international peace building at the grassroots level. At the same time, the book offers conflict resolution scholars and John's fellow practitioners a thoughtful, stimulating analysis of the challenges and techniques associated with a program that seeks to transform perceptions and reconcile long-standing adversaries. *The Enemy Has a Face* has much to contribute to a sophisticated and effective understanding of the process and dynamics of working with youngsters from protracted conflicts.

The United States Institute of Peace's support for Seeds of Peace preceded the fellowship given to the program's founder. Our Grant Program has awarded Seeds of Peace four grants over the past several years, among them one to facilitate development of a CD-ROM (which should be available in the year 2000) that captures the Seeds of Peace experience in words, images, and sounds, and that gives youngsters everywhere the opportunity to share the experience interactively.

As mandated by Congress, the Institute works to promote research, education, and training on approaches to peacefully managing and resolving international conflicts. Since our establishment in 1984, we have supported a great variety of projects that have targeted very different types of conflicts in very different parts of the world. Given the interest of the United States in securing a peaceful Middle East, we have devoted significant attention to that region for more than a decade. In 1999 alone we published Helena Cobban's account of *The Israeli-Syrian Peace Talks: 1991–96 and Beyond;* Adnan Abu-Odeh's insider's look at *Jordanians, Palestinians, and the Hashemite Kingdom in the Middle East Peace Process;* and Arun Elhance's examination of *Hydropolitics in the Third World,* which pays particular attention to conflicts over the waters of the Rivers Jordan, Euphrates, and Tigris; as well as a Special Report, *Thinking Out Loud: Policies toward Iraq.*

The Enemy Has a Face is a most welcome addition to that distinguished list. Despite the bloody trail of international conflict that runs the length of the twentieth century, it is John's, Barbara's, and Tim's achievement—as described in this short volume—to have made the idea of peace seem both plausible and practicable to a generation of young Israelis and Arabs who will become leaders in their own world. For skeptics and idealists alike, this is an inspiring book, a guide to breaking the cycle of generational violence by drawing on that most valuable human resource, the ability of younger generations to see the world anew and to want to create a society of hope to replace an inheritance of hostility and violence.

Richard H. Solomon, President
United States Institute of Peace

ACKNOWLEDGMENTS

The two-year journey that culminated in the publishing of *The Enemy Has a Face* began when Joe Klaits, the director of the United States Institute of Peace's Jennings Randolph Program, asked me if I would be interested in becoming a senior fellow at the Washington, D.C.–based Institute in the fall of 1998. It was inconceivable to me then that I could break away from Seeds of Peace long enough to complete a comprehensive study of the methods we have used since 1993 to help transform a generation of children reared on war to one prepared to wage peace. Joe ignored all my protestations to the contrary and persuaded me that I could tell the story of Seeds of Peace without endangering its future—or my marriage. Without his support and encouragement throughout the ensuing two years, this book would never have been written.

Michael Wallach, coauthor, spent much of his senior year at Cornell University researching conflict resolution with the enduring support of his advisor, Professor Isaac Kramnick. Michael's writings on the process of coexistence, the importance of sharing suffering, the negotiation of symbolic language, and the cathartic effect of camp crises became important chapters of this work. He was also able to reorganize the text to reflect the flow of the camp experience. He thanks the United States Institute of Peace immensely for recognizing his work. It is not often in life that a father has the opportunity to work with his son. I thank Michael for making an enormous contribution to this work and to my life. I could not be prouder.

Sarah Simon, my research assistant, deserves special praise for her hard work. So too does Marieka Van Woerkom, a Dutch cultural anthropologist. Marieka spent hundreds of hours interviewing the Arab and Israeli teenagers throughout the sessions at Seeds of Peace and worked with me at the Institute to transcribe the mountain of interviews and organize them into a workable format. She was an invaluable sounding board for good ideas—and bad—

and has developed into an outstanding facilitator in her own right. I was very fortunate to have Nigel Quinney as the editor of this book. His remarkable skill, adroit suggestions, and insights have made this a far more valuable guide for other groups interested in learning from our experience.

Special mention must be made of Steve Riskin, a program officer in the United States Institute of Peace's Grant Program and a specialist on the Middle East. I hope we have made Steve a believer. His healthy skepticism in our formative years has forced me to take my obligations to this project far more seriously. There are few Middle East scholars who have as much accumulated wisdom or whose perspective is as valuable. Jethro Berkman, a Harvard Divinity School student and a former Dorot scholar in Jerusalem, also provided important material for this book by conducting follow-up interviews with the Israeli and Palestinian participants in Seeds of Peace after they returned to their homes in the Middle East.

Nothing, however, would be possible without the skill and dedication of our facilitators, who have worked year after year under the superb leadership of Linda Carol Pierce, a director of the Family Workshops at NYU's Creative Arts Team. Our nucleus of Israeli and Palestinian facilitators, particularly the teams of Farhat Agbaria and Liat Marcus Gross and Suzanne Khatib and Reuven Barneis, have created an invaluable model for the youngsters. With the opening of our new center in Jerusalem, their teamwork will benefit hundreds, perhaps thousands, of new "Seeds." My special thanks to the talented American facilitators Christopher Lyboldt, Shira Fishkin, Achim Novak, George Anthony, Joel Davidson, Deborah Rager, Sukanya Lahiri, David and Jennifer Allyn, Cynthia Cohen, Janis Astor Del Valle, Elizabeth Friedman, Bill Taylor, and Mark Gammon; to our Russian colleague, Olga Botcharova; and to the Turkish Cypriot and Greek Cypriot team of Sarper Ince and Nicos Anastasiou. There is not enough room to mention all of our counselors, who have given their hearts to this program, but I want to salute head counselors Jerry Smith, Nina Goodman, Larry Malm, and Leslie Adelson. Lindsay Miller, our government and diplomatic liaison, deserves special thanks.

Finally, no one could work with a more dedicated staff in New York than Meredith Katz, Sue Kraglievich, Adam Shapiro, and Marieka Van Woerkom; in Washington Leslie Adelson and Chris Covey; and in Jerusalem Ned Lazarus, Falestin Shehadeh, Sammi Al Jundi, and Roy Sharone. Two special people have shared this vision with me from the early days: Barbara Gottschalk, our executive vice president, and Tim Wilson, our camp director. Together they have inspired an entire generation to move from war to peace. Special thanks too to Aaron Miller, a senior State Department official and true peacemaker who has always believed in our dream.

I am particularly indebted to Richard Solomon. A distinguished diplomat, a sensitive scholar, and a respected leader, Dick was one of the first to understand the importance of Seeds of Peace. Presidents and secretaries of state have relied on his wisdom. So too have these grateful authors.

The Enemy Has a Face

The very first step we have to take right now is not only to want for your own people but to really want, really desire for the other. I mean that if you're an Israeli you have to want for all the Palestinians to be happy and feel safe and feel comfortable. If you're a Palestinian you have to really want for all the Israelis to be happy and feel safe and feel comfortable. You have to really, really want for everyone else to be happy.

—An Arab Seed of Peace, 1996

It took time, but we the wall eventually began to fall. Walls of mighty stones erected from my feelings, from what I understood about my life too early. Stones that I made and built, and I can break them. I started pushing. My will, my capability is what cracked the wall, what rearranged the stones, and made a bridge from them, because I understood that my stones are ruled by me—I can make the wall rise and my will is the power to make it fall.

—An Israeli Seed of Peace, 1997

They learn how to listen to someone else complete their sentence even if the sentence is hurtful. They learn to hear what the other person is trying to say about their needs and their fears and their beliefs. Usually when people begin such a conversation they try to win. Our aim is to change the objective to really understanding the other person as if they are the other person—as if they could step right into that person's life and know exactly how that person feels and why.

—Barbara Gottschalk, Executive Vice President of Seeds of Peace

Introduction

When everything started, I felt very confused. It felt like my mind was divided into two parts. One part felt protected and secure when I saw the soldiers and tanks getting ready to go into the territories. That part of me felt that we should teach the Palestinians a lesson and show them how powerful we are. But there was another part, a part that was created only after our involvement with Seeds of Peace, that felt that what was happening was wrong—that war is wrong. That part knew that there must be another way, a better way. But most of the people don't have a second part. I pray that our leaders have that second part. I know Rabin did.

—AN ISRAELI SEED OF PEACE, 1998

Every summer four hundred Arab and Israeli teenagers from the Middle East descend on a pine-covered crescent thousands of miles away, a camp carved out of the woods in a two-hundred-year-old town in central Maine. The setting, along the shores of Pleasant Lake, is peaceful and harmonious. Its natural beauty is a striking contrast to the climate of conflict they have left behind—fear, the daily threat of violence, the sterile poverty of refugee camps. They arrive at the Seeds of Peace International Camp in Otisfield, Maine, tired and confused, armed with old stereotypes of one another. Some are ready to dismiss the prejudice. "We want to make peace," they say, and smile at the strangers in their midst. Some hold on all too tightly to the stereotypes, too afraid to get into their pajamas the first night, bracing themselves to defend their land and their country against a people they see only as the enemy.

But as they are led to their bunks on the first night, the youngsters begin a three-week process that will turn all of this upside down. They are instantly thrown together—forced to live in the same bunks as their enemies, to eat at the same tables, to shower in the same bathrooms, and to tell one another what often are the same hurtful thoughts. Every day they are forced to be friends and enemies—teammates on the fields and open, honest, forthright peers in daily "coexistence discussions." And just three weeks later, many have undergone profound changes. They stay up talking until the last hours. They tell each other their closest secrets. They e-mail back and forth constantly once home. They are now friends with those who once were their enemies, and spokespeople for a peace they once dismissed. What is it about this experience that changes them so dramatically? Why is it that so many are able to throw away years of built-up aggression, malice, and prejudice? What let Daniel, the Israeli quoted at the start of this chapter, develop this "second part"?

When I created this program in 1993, I worked out of the Hearst Newspapers office in Washington. I was a correspondent, their foreign affairs editor, an author on the Middle East and an occasional television panelist, and happy doing what I did. But years spent reporting on war left me exasperated by violence and eager for peace. The catalyst for Seeds of Peace was the World Trade Center bombing in February 1993. It marked the first time that Americans were targets of fundamentalist terrorists. What was their motive? The answer was clear—to instill fear in the hearts of ordinary Americans, to send the message that there would be a price for continuing American support for Israel and the price would be American lives. For the first time in more than three decades of being a journalist, of having covered four wars in the Middle East and the intifada, the Palestinian uprising against Israeli rule, I asked myself a question: How could we respond to the fear that terrorists try to inculcate? Could we, I wondered, send a message of hope by bringing together the next generation of Arabs and Israelis at an age when they could bond and learn to overcome the fears, prejudices, and inhibitions of their parents and grandparents?

Fortunately I knew a number of the leaders of the Middle East from my days as a journalist. I was one of fourteen reporters who had traveled on former secretary of state Henry Kissinger's plane during most of his Middle East shuttles following the October 1973 war between Israel and its Arab neighbors. These diplomatic missions laid the basis for the initial Egyptian-Israeli troop withdrawals in the Sinai and for the 1978 Camp

David accords that led to the signing of an Israeli-Egyptian treaty of peace. In the course of covering Kissinger's negotiations with Egypt, Israel, Jordan, Syria, and Saudi Arabia, I became acquainted with their leaders, particularly Israel's Yitzhak Rabin and Shimon Peres, Egypt's Anwar Sadat, and Jordan's King Hussein. My newspaper stories and daily reports on the BBC World Service were read and heard in the United States and in the region. In 1980, Janet, my wife, and I also produced and co-wrote a PBS documentary, "Israel and the Palestinians: Will Reason Prevail?" that was praised for presenting Palestinians as people, not merely as terrorists.

A few years later, during the intifada, we wrote a book together, *Still Small Voices*, that sought to portray the lives—and fears—of ordinary Israelis and Palestinians living so close to and yet so far from one another on the Israeli-occupied West Bank of the Jordan River. For several months, we lived with Israelis in their West Bank settlements and with Palestinians in their refugee camps. The book was an effort to help Israelis hear the voices of ordinary Palestinians and an effort to help Palestinians hear the voices of ordinary Israelis. Publication of *Still Small Voices* in 1988 led to yet another project, a biography of Yasser Arafat, at the time probably the most hated "terrorist" in the world. Our motive was not to take sides. We wanted to write a book that would help people understand Arafat and thus help end the ridicule and dehumanization of a man with whom, we believed, Israel would have to deal to make peace. In the course of spending several months in Tunis, the headquarters of the exiled Palestine Liberation Organization (PLO), we were granted unprecedented access to Arafat and his family, friends, and foes in Damascus, Amman, Cairo, and Jerusalem. So by the time *Arafat: In the Eyes of the Beholder* was published in 1990, we were reasonably well known to both the Israeli and the Palestinian leaderships. Indeed, while we were writing the biography, Yitzhak Rabin, who was then the Israeli defense minister, arranged to meet with us secretly in Tel Aviv to quiz us about his nemesis, the PLO chairman, to whom the Israeli would reluctantly offer his hand in friendship only three years later.

Seeds of Peace was born in March 1993 at a dinner party in Washington, D.C., hosted by the indefatigable Esther Coopersmith, a Democratic Party stalwart and goodwill ambassador who has been on a first-name basis with almost every president since Lyndon Johnson. At the dinner honoring Israeli foreign minister Shimon Peres, I asked Esther if I could make a toast. "John privately asked Peres first, would Israel be willing to send youngsters to a peace camp in the United States?" recalled Coopersmith. "'Yes, why not?' Peres replied. Then John made his toast, announcing Seeds of Peace. He challenged Sayed Ahmed al Maher, the Egyptian ambassador, to agree too. He was so embarrassed he said yes," added Coopersmith. When I called Hasan Abdul Rahman, the head of the PLO office in Washington, D.C., he also agreed to send Palestinian teenagers from the West Bank and Gaza. "The next day John publicly proposed it and issued a press release so nobody could back out of it," said Coopersmith. Meanwhile, I prevailed on Joel Bloom, the owner of Camp Powhatan, where my son Michael had spent some of the best summers of his life, to let me use the campsite for the last week of August and the first week of September.

The initial negotiations with the three governments were not easy. I remember an exchange with an official in Jerusalem who told me that thirteen-year-old Israelis were far too young to leave home and attend a camp so far away. "They are not politically mature," the official said. That, of course, was why I wanted them in their early teens—before the combined pressures of parents and grandparents, governments, school systems, and the media had programmed them too politically. Eventually I succeeded in persuading each government to send a small delegation of teenagers to the woods of Maine. The organizational and fund-raising tasks were equally formidable. Fortunately, at a book club evening in Bethesda, Maryland, where Janet and I were invited to discuss the Arafat biography, I met a wonderful woman, a social worker with extensive experience and a deep commitment to Arab-Israeli peace. When I mentioned that I was getting Seeds of Peace off the ground and needed help, Barbara (Bobbie) Gottschalk immediately volunteered. The rest, as they say, is history. Barbara has been at my side ever since. Today, she directs the coexistence (conflict resolution) program that is an important element of Seeds of Peace. The other indispensable member of our initial team was Tim Wilson, a schoolteacher and former football coach who was codirector of Camp Powhatan's regular summer season for American campers. Tim, a veteran leader of the civil rights movement, was the first African American to head the human rights division of the state of Maine. He is one of the most inspirational figures I have ever met. His physique, not to mention his out-wardly tough demeanor born of decades of counseling high school victims of drive-by shootings in his native Pittsburgh, gives Tim the stature of some-one, as the campers say, "you don't mess with." With Barbara and Tim, I set out to raise the initial $25,000 to get the first Seeds of Peace season off the ground.

There was, and is, a method to my madness. Above all, it is vital that camp life reflect a neutral, loving, and supportive environment. As you will see, for many of these youngsters, simply living together under the same roof can be traumatic. In the first few days of camp, the things that we take for granted with our friends—eating our meals together and playing baseball, soccer, or tennis—can be frightening and formidable with people you have been schooled to hate. Removing the image of the "other" as an enemy is indispensable in beginning to create the structure for trust and understanding. Terry Anderson, the Associated Press reporter who was the longest-held American hostage in Lebanon, told me shortly after he was released: "John, if you achieve nothing else, at least the enemy will have a face." Accepting the "other" as nonthreatening is the initial goal when the youngsters arrive at Seeds of Peace. When that happens, a sense of community begins to be created that gives everyone a stake in its welfare—and survival. With it comes a new sense of safety that permits the "Seeds" to relax and open up to one another in the vital daily meetings we dub "coexistence sessions."

Our first summer, in 1993, was for boys only. The Egyptian government and the Palestinian authorities had cautioned us that it was too soon to bring women, particularly young women, to a camp in the United States where they would live together with young men. Not merely Muslim fundamentalists but most parents would frown on any suggestion of communal living—even if the girls were strictly separated and lived in different bunks that were isolated from the boys' part of camp. So in our first year we were 45 boys: 20 Israelis, 15 Palestinians, and 10 Egyptians. Although we wanted to include women, it might not have happened until much later had it not been for pressure from Barbra Streisand. She saw the first group of "Seeds" on television at the historic 1993 White House signing of the Israeli-Palestinian Declaration of Principles and offered us badly needed funding—but only if we would include young women in the program. Surprisingly, the same governments that warned us not to do so ultimately agreed to include women in their 1994 delegations. For our part, in addition to carefully monitored separate housing, we agreed to provide separate swimming facilities, and to facilitate prayer services for the Muslims every Friday afternoon and for the Jews every Friday evening. Today, the delegations chosen by each government reflect a 50:50 balance between boys and girls. Among the Israeli and Arab delegations there are even several religiously orthodox youngsters whose special dietary and other needs are provided for every summer.

The composition of the total camp population is designed so that approximately 40 percent of the campers are Israeli and 50 percent of the Arabs are Palestinian. In that way, the Israelis and Palestinians make up two-thirds of the total number of campers that average between 160 and 180 per each three-week session. Seeds of Peace now schedules three sessions every summer, which permits us to reach more than three hundred new campers every summer and to enlist the help of one hundred youngsters from previous summers to assume peer support and program leader responsibilities. In recent years, Seeds of Peace has begun separate program for teenagers from other war zones, including Cyprus, the Balkans, and southern Europe. The focus of this book, however, reflects the main focus of our work: our Middle East program.

Today, nine governments actively participate in Seeds of Peace: Cyprus (north and south), Egypt, Israel, Jordan, Morocco, the Palestinian National Authority, Qatar, Tunisia, and Yemen. In order to allow each government an opportunity to build a group that is acceptable to its constituency and accountable to its people, we ask every government to select its own delegation of teenagers and accompanying adult leaders. No funding is sought from any participating government. However, Seeds of Peace recommends general criteria for the selection process: teenagers should be chosen through the educational system (public and private schools) and have a working knowledge of the English language. Each teenage applicant is expected to write an essay on some aspect of the Arab-Israeli conflict that is evaluated by the respective ministries. Seeds of Peace suggests that the final group of candidates be interviewed in English to test their language skills.

Having the governments select their participants gives each delegation an official imprimatur that is important to the goals of Seeds of Peace. But even more important, the governments' hands-on involvement has helped ensure that those selected are not chiefly from families that are already ideologically disposed to liberal or dovish causes. Thus, when a right-wing government was elected in Israel in 1996, the composition of the Israeli delegation reflected the more hawkish views of the governing Likud coalition that had assumed power. The Palestinian delegation includes a sizable number of refugee camp youngsters because the government feels a need to be accountable to the poor as well as to the more middle-class segments of Palestinian society. These teenagers also tend to be more hawkish in their attitudes. This is as it should be. The mission of Seeds of Peace is to help humanize a conflict that has thrived partly because both sides have so successfully dehumanized each other. It is important for us to receive as many youngsters from right-wing or conservative backgrounds as from more tolerant or liberal perspectives.

It costs Seeds of Peace approximately $2,500 for each youngster's three-and-a-half-week stay in the United States, not including airfare. Each family is asked to contribute $1,200 to help defray the cost of the round-trip air travel, but, once chosen, no one is excluded if his or her family cannot afford it. Each government also knows that it can offer scholarships for the entire or partial cost of the airfare to anyone who genuinely needs one.

The final composition of each delegation reflects the nature of each government. The Israelis and the Palestinians have done an exemplary job of democratically choosing their delegations from a broad political, social, and economic spectrum and generally without regard to privilege. There are exceptions. In 1994, when the Labor Government led by Yitzhak Rabin was in power, a right-wing member of the Knesset (the Israeli Parliament) attacked the government for selecting teenagers from families that were known Labor Party supporters. It was discovered only later that his own son had been denied a place in the delegation.

The Jordanian and Egyptian selection process reflects those countries' keen desire to ensure that their best and brightest represent their nation abroad. Since English is taught primarily at English-language schools in Egypt, generally attended by the elite of the society, the selection of the Egyptian youngsters has reflected less of a cross-section than in other delegations. In Jordan, the delegation was initially chosen from students attending the Jubilee School established by Her Majesty Queen Noor al-Hussein to ensure that gifted Jordanian youngsters, regardless of their economic or social status, receive a head start in their education. In 1999, Their Majesties King Abdullah II and Queen Rania further democratized the selection process, broadening the delegation to include teenagers from every political and social strata of Jordanian society. Although Seeds of Peace constantly urges all governments to broaden the selection process, nations joining the program for the first time tend to restrict the selection. Thus, it came as no surprise that in its first year of sending teenagers, Yemen sent the son of its foreign minister and a nephew of the prime minister.

In general, Seeds of Peace is not involved in the selection process. However, certain situations have required us to weigh in. For example, the Israeli government was initially reluctant to include in its delegation as many Israeli Arabs as one would expect given the percentage of Arabs (approximately 18 percent) who are citizens of Israel.

Seeds of Peace, in coordination with the respective governments, selects the delegates who return for a second or third summer. They are chosen on the basis of their participation in Seeds of Peace activities in the region, their overall leadership skills, and an essay that each is asked to write on why they believe they should come back. It is, however, becoming more and more difficult to select these peer support and program leaders. With the growing numbers of graduates, we cannot bring back all of the deserving candidates. To help meet the need to continually challenge our graduates, we have developed new programs such as the Novartis Youth Summit (similar to model high school programs run by the United Nations) that allow us to bring as many as one hundred teenage alumni to Switzerland every year. At these summits, the older graduates are asked to use the listening and other skills they learned at Seeds of Peace in actual political negotiations—for example, in drafting a final Israeli-Palestinian peace treaty.

Relations with the governments often are as complex as the Arab-Israeli negotiations themselves. At times governments have even sought to use the youngsters as pawns to punish an action taken by the "other side." In the summer of 1994, only a week before the opening of the Seeds of Peace Camp, Israeli troops launched massive retaliatory raids in Lebanon, bombing Hezbollah guerrilla camps and killing a number of civilians. In response, an Arab government declared that it would not be sending a delegation to Seeds of Peace. But the youngsters' families refused to be intimidated. They declared that they were sending their children anyway. Less than twenty-four hours before the start of camp, the government backed down and the delegation arrived a day late but without incident.

From 1996 to 1999, when Israeli prime minister Benjamin Netanyahu pointedly refused to recognize Palestinian statehood, Seeds of Peace came under Israeli pressure to stop using the term "Palestine" in any public ceremonies, publications, or activities. In 1997, in a move to signal its displeasure with the fact that Palestinian teenagers were permitted to say they came from "Palestine," the Ministry of Education, headed by Yitzhak Levy, a member of the orthodox National Religious Party, deliberately delayed sending the names of the Israeli delegation. After the exchange of several drafts, a compromise was reached preserving the right of the Palestinians to say they come from Palestine—but committing Seeds of Peace to follow the practice of the host country, the United States of America, in using the name of the government, the Palestinian National Authority, instead of the yet-to-be-declared nation, Palestine. In this book, too, we will use the name of the government, except of course when we quote the youngsters themselves or recount their discussions about Palestine.

Less than four months after I met Barbara Gottschalk, our first camp began to take shape. Seeds of Peace was an idea that seemed to make sense: Bring the next generation together before they too fall victim to the hate that ensnares their parents and grandparents—bring them together and see what happens. What happened was that after one summer, I became so convinced that this was the only way to break the unending cycles of violence that I seriously considered quitting my job as a nationally syndicated correspondent. I had covered the Arab-Israeli conflict at close range for almost three decades. Seeds of Peace seemed to be the way to be on the front lines of resolving the conflict. The opportunity arose at the end of our second summer, in 1994. I had invited Nobel Laureate Elie Wiesel to speak during our tour of the Holocaust Museum in Washington, D.C. Elie was moved by the sight of 150 Arab and Israeli youngsters sharing the pain and suffering that he had experienced as a child in the Nazi concentration camps. In his remarks in the auditorium, he mentioned that my name in Hebrew meant "a gift from God." Then he announced that if I ever wanted to leave my journalism career, he would offer me a position as executive director of his foundation in New York. After he concluded, I asked him if he was serious. He suggested that I contact Arnold Thaler, the deeply motivated vice president of the Elie Wiesel Foundation for Humanity. Arnold spent the next several months recruiting me for the position. In February 1995, I finally decided to retire from having to meet daily deadlines. Janet and I sold our home and our American folk art collection and moved to New York, ready to take on the challenge of administering a foundation and, in my spare time, shepherding Seeds of Peace into a new era of growth. As Seeds of Peace grew, so did my preoccupation with its welfare. In the spring of 1997, I asked Elie to be relieved from my duties at the foundation so that I could devote my entire life to raising the funds for the expansion of Seeds of Peace. I am eternally grateful to Elie, his wife, Marion, and Arnold Thaler for the opportunity they gave me to make the transition to a new career. Seven years and almost one thousand five hundred teenagers later, Seeds of Peace has changed almost every life it has touched— most profoundly my own.

Over the years we have learned something about the processes that these youngsters go through during the three weeks of camp. We have come to understand when and where they need to be supported and when and where they need to be pushed. We are beginning to understand and expect the phases of change and the patterns of confidence and confusion that are steps in their journey toward mutual understanding. We see the same recurring arguments, how they haunt us again and again, and why it is as important for the youngsters to engage in these arguments as it is for them to find solutions to both their personal and ideological conflicts.

The Seeds of Peace experience raises a lot of questions: How do these youngsters change, and why? What do we do to support them? What are the chief difficulties and challenges we face? What are the chief difficulties they face? Can bringing people together for three weeks really have a lasting effect in the region at large? This book addresses these questions by tracing the various stages and identifying the key elements within a Seeds of Peace program.

We begin in chapter 1 with the youngsters' arrival at camp and the efforts made to create a supportive, open environment in which they can think and speak for themselves. Chapter 2 examines the kinds of stereotypes of one another they bring with them and then describes how these are gradually broken down to allow personal friendships to grow. In chapter 3 we focus on the daily "coexistence discussions," two-hour facilitation sessions that give the campers the opportunity to work through the history, symbols, and suffering of both sides in the conflict. In chapter 4 we see how a crisis at camp serves to disrupt but then to deepen the relationships that have been established among the youngsters. The camp experience culminates in the Color Games, which, as chapter 5 describes, divide the entire camp into two multinational teams for a host of competitions. The youngsters' return home is chronicled in chapter 6, which explores the difficulties that arise as families and friends react with surprise and often scorn to the new ideas and new relationships that the campers have brought home with them. Chapter 7 outlines some of the steps that Seeds of Peace has taken to help our graduates stay in contact with one another and to continue the work they began at camp. Finally, chapter 8 offers some concluding thoughts on how and why the youngsters change and what this suggests to a world still searching for ways to build peace.

Although we work hard to make each program a success, it is clearly the youngsters who change themselves. And although we try to help the returning campers develop the ideas they have initiated in Maine, in the end the youngsters themselves do the hard and courageous work of making peace with one another. Seeds of Peace is not about planting trees or singing songs. Although Seeds of Peace takes place at a summer camp, we are not a traditional summer camp program. The natural setting of the camp allows the basic human instincts to surface in a safe and secure environment where young people can get to know one another as human beings. But Seeds of Peace, above all, is about making real peace in the real world. It is about changing attitudes, ending the fears and prejudices that have prevented entire generations from getting to know one another; in short, it is about "rehumanizing," not dehumanizing, the enemy. No one tells this story better than the youngsters themselves. As much as possible, I have let them tell their story as they experienced it so that the reader will feel some of their frustrations and anger and, ultimately, hope. Many of the quotations are transcriptions from the coexistence sessions as well as from subsequent interviews that allowed the youngsters to reflect on the changes they were experiencing. (Most transcriptions are verbatim, but on occasion grammatical mistakes have been corrected for the sake of clarity.)

"My goal became to understand Israelis," said Hazem, a Jordanian youngster. "I had always seen them as bad and even thought they knew themselves to be bad. This is not the case. I discovered that the history they believe to be true justifies much of what has been done by them, as the history I believe to be true justifies much of what Arabs have done." For Hazem, like so many others, the personal experience of getting to know the other side is the most memorable. "I've been stranded with an Israeli on a sailboat in the middle of the lake because the wind stopped blowing. I have been in canoes with Israelis on more than one occasion; I was saved from burning myself when an Israeli saw that the tray of hot gravy I was carrying was about to tip over." What is Hazem most proud of? He says, "I have slept next to Israelis for a total of more than two months and never found reason to be worried. Seeds of Peace may be the only place where an Israeli will truly want an Arab to score in an Israeli goalkeeper's net and vice versa."

As their comments reveal, their journey from fear and suspicion to understanding and trust is twisting and difficult. They often find themselves heading down dead-end streets, doubling back on themselves, wishing they had never chosen such a journey at all. Yet, eventually, most reach their destination: a new level of compassion for one another as human beings. When they return home, they are well on their way to becoming the true leaders of a new generation that is as committed to fighting for peace as their predecessors were in waging war.

Arrival

1

Building a Community

Each year, our Middle East program brings together four hundred Arab and Israeli boys and girls who have been selected by their governments from more than two thousand applicants. Since the Israeli-Palestinian struggle has generally been considered to be at the heart of the Arab-Israeli conflict (see the feature box on pages 16–21), the two largest delegations, making up approximately two-thirds of the total camp population, are the Israeli and the Palestinian groups. The entire cost of the three-week session in the United States is borne by Seeds of Peace. It is raised from year-round events hosted by Jewish American and Arab American families in the United States, from generous corporate and foundation donors, and from several thousand ordinary American citizens who each year graciously contribute whatever they can to support us. The delegations are composed of youngsters from settlements and refugee camps, from families of aristocrats and families of war heroes, from the homes of Holocaust victims and refugees.

A Short History of the Arab-Israeli Conflict

It is helpful to view the Israeli-Palestinian struggle as less of a conflict between right and wrong than a battle between two rights. At its essence, the Arab-Israeli conflict is about two peoples who have refused throughout their common history to recognize each other—as a people, a nation, or a nationality. These two peoples, the Arabs and the Israelis, have fought throughout the latter half of the twentieth century to deny each other the basic human, civil, and political rights and privileges that each demands for itself.

But their conflict goes back much further, into the prehistorical era when the Bible says that both peoples descended from the progeny of a common father, Abraham. God promised one of his sons, Isaac, "all the land of Canaan for an everlasting possession" (Genesis 17:8). He made a similar promise to his other son, the first-born Ishmael. He told Ishmael that he would also make of his descendants "a great nation" (Genesis 16:12). Indeed, the Israeli-Palestinian struggle is a fight over the same land—between the Mediterranean Sea and the Jordan River—the land that both peoples claim as their ancestral homeland. Each people has known its share of suffering, the loss of its homeland, and the passionate desire to return to it. After the Jews fled from their bondage in Egypt, they conquered the Land of Canaan and ruled Hebron, where Abraham was buried, and the highlands of what is today the West Bank for more than a thousand years. This is the same land—called Judea and Samaria by religious Jews—to which Abraham migrated with his flocks from Mesopotamia and where today many Israeli zealots have estab-

Participating governments

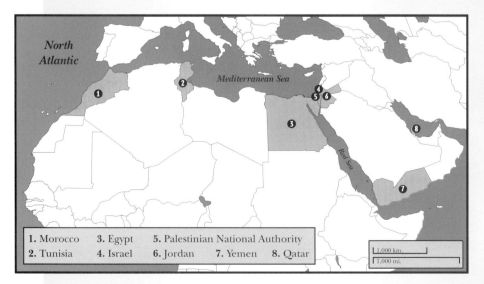

1. Morocco 3. Egypt 5. Palestinian National Authority
2. Tunisia 4. Israel 6. Jordan 7. Yemen 8. Qatar

lished settlements in an attempt to affirm the biblical connection. These holy lands for ultra-religious Jews are only a small part of the West Bank—so called because it lies on the western bank of the Jordan River (the eastern bank borders the Hashemite Kingdom of Jordan). The West Bank, however, is also the land to which hundreds of thousands of Arab refugees fled after Israel was created in 1948—and where their extended families are living today. These refugees, and their descendents, are today's Palestinians. Their population in the West Bank and Gaza Strip today is close to two million people.

For Palestinians and many non-Arab historians, the word "Palestine" goes back as far in prehistory as the Jews themselves. Palestinians trace their roots to the Philistines, a people of Greek origin who settled on the coastal plains of the Mediterranean and who, the Palestinians assert, were subjugated by the Jews (who took over the interior) until the year 66 C.E., when the Jews revolted against the Romans. The Romans, intent on eliminating the Jews, not only destroyed the Second Temple, the Temple of Solomon in Jerusalem, but renamed the territory "Syria Palestina" (after the Jews' two other greatest enemies) and moved its political center to Damascus. Most Jews were sold into slavery or were scattered throughout the Roman Empire. Jewish prayers and literature ever since have called for a return to the site of the Second Temple in Jerusalem.

In 1897, motivated by an upsurge in anti-Semitism in Europe, an Austrian journalist, Theodor Herzl, founded a movement calling for a return to Zion (Jerusalem). Zionism soon became the major motivating force of Jews seeking a safe, secure home. In 1917, Lord Balfour, the British foreign secretary, promised a homeland to the Jews partly in response to pleas from British Zionists to save the Jews who were being slaughtered in pogroms in Russia and Eastern Europe. But Great Britain, immersed in World War I and seeking to secure Arab support for its fight against the Ottoman Turks in the Middle East, also promised a homeland in Palestine to the Sharif Hussein of Mecca, the leader of the populous Hashemite clan in Arabia. Palestinian self-identity in the twentieth century began as a reaction to the influx of tens of thousands of Jews into Palestine at the turn of the century.

After World War I, with the Ottoman Empire now destroyed, the League of Nations gave Great Britain a mandate to administer Palestine and direct its future. Throughout the 1930s and 1940s, British forces in Mandatory Palestine became the targets of attacks by both Arabs and Jews, who were angry that the promises made during World War I had not been kept. The

Arabs also were angry that Jews escaping persecution in Europe were immigrating in record numbers to Palestine. In 1914, the Jews in Palestine accounted for less than 15 percent of the total population (85,000 Jews were living among 600,000 Muslim and Christian Arabs). By 1947, the Jewish presence in Palestine had grown to almost half of the total population (600,000 Jews were living among a population of 1.3 million). In 1939, Britain officially gave notice to the United Nations that it would withdraw its forces from Palestine and end its mandate within ten years. The Nazi extermination of six million Jews in World War II added impetus for the United Nations to act to help the Jews and the Arabs establish states of their own. In 1948, the land was partitioned into an Arab and a Jewish homeland. Jerusalem was declared an international zone to be administered by the United Nations.

However, the Arabs who had been living in historic Palestine since the Arab Conquest in 637 C.E. saw no reason why they should suffer for the crimes of the Nazis. Consequently the Arabs refused the UN offer of partition and on May 15, 1948, the day after the Jews declared themselves independent in their part of the former British mandate, five Arab states declared war on Israel. In the ensuing violence, Israel defeated the armies of Transjordan, Syria, Lebanon, Iraq, and Egypt and conquered West Jerusalem, the only Palestinian area where Jews had been a majority. The West Bank of the Jordan River and East Jerusalem came under the control of Transjordan, which in 1950 renamed itself the Hashemite Kingdom of Jordan.

After the Arab armies were routed by Jewish forces, 133,000 Arabs remained in Israel and eventually were granted citizenship with limited rights. But approximately 500,000 had fled in fear for their lives to the West Bank and Gaza Strip, longing to return to their homes in what was now a Jewish state. In the wake of this exodus, the modern Palestinian nationalist movement was born. With the neighboring Arab nations reluctant to fight Israel again until they had strengthened their armies, Palestinians became increasingly frustrated and angry. The Palestine Liberation Organization (PLO), which was formed by the Egyptian government to try to placate Palestinian frustrations, turned into a mouthpiece for Ahmed Shukeiry, an Arab League official whose anti-Israeli oratory made headlines but did little to advance Palestinian aspirations. In the fall of 1964 in Kuwait, Yasser Arafat and others founded Fatah, the underground armed branch of the PLO. Fatah began targeting Israelis in hopes that its guerrilla raids would force the Jewish state to retaliate against its Arab neighbors, which would in turn provoke Arab leaders into a major new war to destroy Israel (an avowed aim in the PLO Covenant).

The tactics succeeded in sparking another war in June 1967, when Israel engaged the armies of Egypt, Jordan, Syria, and Iraq. This time the Israeli armies routed the Arabs in six days, taking control of the West Bank and East Jerusalem from Jordan, the Golan Heights from Syria, and the Sinai Peninsula and Gaza Strip from Egypt. Israel unified the eastern and western sectors of Jerusalem and declared the city its eternal capital. Following the war, the Labor government in Israel also authorized Jews to settle among the hundreds of thousands of Palestinians in the Israeli-occupied West Bank and Gaza Strip. Security was the major reason for the first settlements. Low-cost mortgages were provided to Jews to settle on the highest ridges of the West Bank so that these heavily fortified hilltops could become a buffer against new Arab attacks. But another group of settlers now began moving, at first surreptitiously, into the Palestinian territories. These were the religiously fundamentalist Jews who believed that the lightning nature of the Israeli victory was a sign from God that they were intended to reclaim the biblical lands that were once part of ancient Judea and Samaria.

After the Labor government was defeated in 1976 by the rightist Likud coalition, led by Menachem Begin's Herut party, settlements began to grow in both number and size. They were encouraged by the new Israeli government, which openly sought to move hundreds of thousands of Jews onto Arab-inhabited land.

Israel and its neighbors

Israel repressed any manifestation of Palestinian nationality or statehood with increasing severity over the next two decades. Thousands of alleged Palestinian terrorists were arrested and imprisoned, and tales of torture and mistreatment grew increasingly common. Finally, in December 1987, West Bank Palestinians took matters into their own hands. They began launching fierce attacks with stones, Molotov cocktails, and whatever rudimentary weapons they could fashion to rid themselves of the Israeli occupiers. This became known as the "intifada," the Palestinian uprising, and it forced Arafat to make new efforts from PLO headquarters in Tunis to negotiate a better future for the Palestinians.

The Gulf crisis and war of 1990–91, however, proved a setback for the PLO, which openly sided with Iraq against the U.S.-led coalition to oust Iraqi forces from Kuwait. The coalition included Arab states such as Saudi Arabia and Syria, which had traditionally supported the PLO, but which cut off Palestinian subsidies in light of the PLO's pro-Iraqi stance. Aware that the PLO was weakened in Arab and international circles, the Israeli prime minister, Yitzhak Rabin, and Shimon Peres, his foreign minister, authorized the beginning of secret, low-level talks with the PLO in Oslo. The PLO was still an outlaw organization in Israel, but two of Peres's closest aides, Yossi Beilin and Uri Savir, were sitting directly across the table from Arafat's own lieutenants. These secret negotiations went on for almost a year and finally produced agreement on an Israeli-Palestinian Declaration of Principles (DOP). The DOP was signed on the South Lawn of the White House on September 13, 1993. Prodded by President Clinton, Rabin reluctantly shook Arafat's hand and signed the first accord that recognized the PLO as the sole and legitimate representative of the Palestinian people. The pact promised an immediate Israeli pullout from Jericho, an ancient Arab town near the Jordanian border, and Gaza, a densely populated Arab area on the Israeli border with Egypt. The DOP also recognized the rights that each of their peoples had to live in peace in contiguous homelands. This, in turn, led to the creation of the Palestinian National Authority, the first Palestinian government to exercise authority and control in the parts of the West Bank from which Israel agreed to pull out its troops and end its twenty-six-year occupation.

The agreement set the stage for a series of Israeli withdrawals over the next three years that resulted in Gaza becoming the seat of the new Palestinian government. Over the next five years Palestinians gradually gained control over more than a third of the territory of the West Bank, including Nablus, Ramallah, parts of Hebron, and other cities and towns that had a majority Arab population. But the most difficult controversies over Palestinian statehood, the "right of return" or of compensation for several million Palestinian refugees, and the future of the vastly expanded Jewish settlements—and Jerusalem itself—remained for future negotiations. Rabin's assassination in 1995 by a fanatic right-wing settler and the subsequent election of the more hawkish Netanyahu government in Israel created a stalemate in the peace process that did not become unglued until summer 1999.

In June, Israeli voters turned Netanyahu out of power and elected as prime minister Ehud Barak, the leader of the Labor Party and the most decorated soldier in Israeli history. Barak prided himself above all on being a protégé of Yitzhak Rabin. He vowed to give new impetus to the peace talks, promising he would work alongside Arafat instead of simply sitting across the table from him, and pledging to restart talks on an Israeli withdrawal from the Syrian Golan Heights. Hopes were thus rekindled that a Palestinian state would finally come into existence through a nonviolent, evolutionary process. In a major agreement signed on September 5 in Egypt, Barak and Arafat vowed to conclude negotiations on a final settlement by September 2000.

The tortured history of the Arab-Israeli conflict and the pain suffered by both sides punctuate almost all the discussions held between the delegations at camp. Indeed, the respective governments prepare their teenagers to continue the ideological struggle fought for generations by their leaders. Governments view the program as coaches might a soccer game—they coach their side to win. This attitude colors the selection process, with youngsters being chosen not merely for their English-language facility but also for their ability to defend their nation's policies and positions. Each government now holds pre-camp retreats, usually lasting for a few days, at which senior officials brief the delegation and caution them not to say anything that might be embarrassing to their people back home. More than one government has warned its delegates that it will know, presumably from other teenagers in the group, if any of them challenge the official position. Thus, one of our greatest challenges is to coax these youngsters to think for themselves. This begins on the first day of camp, at the flag-raising ceremony, and continues through their visit to Washington, D.C., at the end of their stay in the United States.

Each delegation is accompanied to camp by government-appointed chaperones known as "delegation leaders" or "escorts." Barbara Zasloff, a noted psychologist and director of our delegation leader program, schedules numerous activities—including Outward Bound adventures, trips to historic sites, lectures on facets of American democracy, home visits with citizens of nearby Otisfield and Casco—designed to foster close relationships among the delegation leaders. At an American camp, parents are permitted to visit only on two or three designated days every summer. For us, too, it is vital that the Arab and Israeli youngsters have their own space and freedom to interact without adults looking over their shoulder. Over the years we have reached a healthy compromise between the delegation leaders' desire to be with their delegations and the youngsters' need for time to interact with one another. Each delegation leader meets twice a week with his or her entire group and is welcome to share occasional meals with the youngsters and to attend the daily 7:30 A.M. "lineup," when the entire camp gathers at the flagpole outside the "Big Hall."

The other adults at the camp are administrative support staff employed by Seeds of Peace. In addition to Tim Wilson, our camp director, they include forty-six counselors—one for almost every four campers—who are always available to oversee, encourage, and help out the youngsters; fourteen facilitators, who conduct the daily two-hour coexistence sessions; two artists-in-residence; and a variety of other ancillary staff, among them a chef and kitchen crew, a doctor and nurses, and carpentry and ground maintenance staff.

Each youngster comes with his or her own emotional baggage. Many are afraid of one another and refuse to go to sleep the first night—too scared that the youngster next to them will harm them in the dark. Many are used to making fun of one another, and certainly no one is used to playing sports or doing art together. Getting past these initial fears and alienation is one of our most important missions. It takes time, as Amer, a fifteen-year-old Palestinian, recalls:

> At the first moment when we reached the camp, we were so tired, the bus had broken, we were kept waiting until late at night. They put us in the dining hall, and they brought out benches that I didn't like very much. They were full of sand. I thought when they took us to the bunk everyone would choose to sleep next to who they wanted because that's the plan I had. We were four Palestinians who were very close friends, and I said, "Okay, we'll sit together, we'll forget the Israelis." Then we met our counselor Andy, and he said, "Okay, you're with me," and there were two Israelis, and there were two Jordanians, a Moroccan,

a Qatari, and there was me. We started walking to the bunk, and our bunk was the last one in camp, so we kept walking. I was holding my bags and walking, late at night, to the last bunk, and then I saw the showers and everything, and I said, "Oh God, how come I came here?" In the morning I didn't put away my things from my bag. I kept them in my backpack. I didn't trust the Israelis. I put my bags behind my bed.

And then the next day we started to know each other more. In my bunk there was my best Palestinian friend. They called us the twins. We were all the time together. The next day there were bunk activities so we had to go with the Israelis and gradually we knew each other more and more. I had a Jordanian friend called Hazem and another Rami. And I started to be friends with Ya'ir, an Israeli. So we started to be friends and more friends, and by the end of camp now some of my closest friends are from the coexistence sessions. These are the ones that I fought with the most, Tzachi and Inat and Roit. We were always fighting, fighting together, and then we were upside down: friends. At the last session, the facilitator wanted us to talk, and we kept laughing. We said we don't want to go to the coexistence sessions, we want to have fun just alone.

One of our primary goals is to have each youngster create friendships as close as those created by Amer. Another is to allow for the kind of productive arguing that he speaks of—the "fighting" that eventually turns "upside down." For this to happen, we have to provide a safe, neutral, supportive environment in which friendship is regarded as normal; honest expression is supported; courage is validated; self-confidence is primed; and pride is nourished. We try to reverse social norms that keep people apart intellectually, emotionally, and socially. Youngsters must feel that camp is a safe place for them—a place where they can express themselves and reach out to one another without fearing the consequences. Given what the youngsters learn at home in "normal" daily life, ours is a bold ambition; but when it works, Seeds of Peace becomes a real community, a safe community with its own flag, anthem, T-shirts, and smiling faces.

Heaven in Maine

Relocating the students from the Middle East region—from daily hostility and the daily exposure to external threat—to our campsite is critical to creating this sense of community. The siege mentality that exists in the region has left most people on both sides convinced that they are the victims of the other side. It would be nearly impossible to conduct this program in Israel or in the Palestinian territories—one side would always seem psychologically dominant. Conducting the program on neutral ground, on the territory of the nation that, for better or worse, tries to remain an impartial arbiter, creates a sense of fairness that both sides accept.

Shortly after arriving at camp, a fourteen-year-old Palestinian surveyed the shores of Pleasant Lake and the surrounding beauty of the Maine woods and asked, "Have I died and gone to heaven?" Perhaps he was only half joking; the physical distance he had traveled from his Gaza refugee camp may have made it easier for him to transcend the narrow perspectives that imprison him at home. Whether camp is "heaven" or "benches full of sand," it is a place of its own, neutral to all, where we can set the rules.

It is also far away from destructive social pressures, constant media distortion, and textbooks and teachers who are too often a part of the dehumanizing process. After news of a terrorist bombing reached camp, Sivan, an Israeli, said that having Palestinians to console her at camp made a huge difference. "When you're at home, you see what your parents do, what your friends do. My family watches TV and listens to the radio. I can see how my whole country feels and acts, so you adjust yourself to that," she explained.

Seeds of Peace encourages interdelegation social interaction in order to decrease the effects of intradelegation peer pressure to remain separate from the "enemy." All the youngsters at the camp become members of three distinct and smaller groups: their bunk of eight, with whom they sleep; the table of ten, with whom they eat; and their coexistence group of twelve, which meets every day in different parts of the camp. Dozens of sporting and other activities (art and drama, for example) involve larger numbers, but creating the smaller groups permits the youngsters to establish separate havens—safe places where they can make choices and reach out to one another. Each of these smaller units, meanwhile, encourages teamwork and interaction—for instance, the bunks are graded on inspections as a unit, and the eating groups come up with chants that playfully speak to the competitive spirit that camp fosters. Banging on tables during meals is not discouraged as the youngsters then rise with their counselor to cheer for the food or goad the tables around them. At night the bunks come together in the Big Hall, the gym that houses a proscenium stage and a large basketball court, for art competitions and activities such as "dress up your counselor"—silly stuff, but it helps them to become a group, a team.

The traditional American camp experience is thus invaluable to our program. Eating meals together, sleeping in the same bunks, and playing on the same soccer team do not constitute peace. But they are effective steps toward creating a sense of normalcy, toward establishing a climate in which few question or even think about the fact that they are involved in games with the same people their societies often denounce as "subhuman."

It is important that everyone speak the same language. English is required for entrance to the program and is the only language allowed at the camp. This rule is strictly enforced to ensure that everyone knows what is being said at all times, and thus to forestall any suspicions of plots being hatched or insults hidden in an alien tongue. When the rule is broken by the campers, who can slip into their native tongue easily, they are immediately asked to translate what they have said. It is important for the campers to know that one side is not reverting to Hebrew or Arabic to plot against the other. The use of English also is a unifying psychological tool that helps to reinforce the fact that Seeds of Peace is an American institution.

Counselors are also encouraged to break up cliques of Arab or Israeli youngsters, who naturally find it more comfortable to share their private views with their own people. It is easy to stay with one's own, and it can be a difficult experience for a teenager to reach out to another and form a trusting relationship. So Seeds of Peace begins its support at the very first moments, often well past midnight, when the buses pull through the gates and the exhausted and frightened campers dismount with their weighty backpacks and seemingly endless amounts of luggage. From that moment, they are "Seeds" of peace. Counselors swarm the buses, warmly welcoming the campers with shouted greetings and hugs. The support continues throughout camp, with the 1:4 ratio of counselors to campers allowing enormous attention to be lavished on each camper. "I spend probably half an hour of every day just giving high fives," said one counselor. The youngsters respond to this. "Kids pull me aside all summer and say, 'Michael, I love you.'" Surrounded by love, it is much easier for youngsters to reach out to one another—to new people and to new ideas. The campers must be willing to say things they would normally be too afraid to share. Only then can they deal with the subtle and often hidden assumptions that underlie their differences. Just as we in our lives share personal stories only in the company of those we love, so do the campers. Knowing they have the support of the counselors and facilitators allows them to take these chances.

Taking Advantage of Adolescence

One of the reasons why Seeds of Peace focuses on teenagers is that they are usually accepting of this kind of support and eager for teamwork. "The central theme of adolescence is finding an identity, a sense of self, in relation to the world," says Stanley Walzer, professor emeritus of child psychiatry at Harvard University's Medical School and former chief of psychiatry at Children's Hospital in Boston who spends his summers at the Seeds of Peace camp. "Although chronic exposure to war may constitute a significant interference with a child's social development, his or her adaptive capacities may mute the more pronounced effects of the stresses. Seeds of Peace builds on the natural resiliency of teenagers to overcome adversity and realize their full developmental potentials." He points to the central role of athletics in the adolescent development of both boys and girls. "Adolescents are physically active and they frequently find themselves in school and community settings that highly value athletics." Sports, says Walzer, are a "language" that everyone understands. "They offer a sense of the familiar in the new and strange environment of the camping situation. Furthermore, they allow the teenagers to participate as members of a team, or individually, on the basis of interests and abilities rather than on political beliefs or ethnic backgrounds."

Camp director Tim Wilson hugs a camper

As products of societies at war, our teenagers already embody many prejudices about one another. Yet they are young enough to change and bold enough to take the emotional risks that their elders cannot. Our immediate impact on the Middle East might be greater if we were able to work with members of the Palestinian and Israeli governments—but aside from the impracticalities of arranging such an exercise, in many ways we can achieve far more with those who are outside the political world. Teenagers do not have to worry that if they share too much the other side may use the information against them. The youngsters may say, for example, that someday they would be willing to share Jerusalem, which both sides claim as their own capital. They can do that without worrying that their statement will be on the front page of tomorrow's newspapers. Their self-identities are rarely bound up with their embrace of particular political positions, so they can craft new perspectives during the program without fearing a loss of their own sense of self or of their reputations. They also tend to trust one another more easily and are more likely to build relationships during recreational activities that can be trusted later, during political discussions, to deliver honesty and forthrightness.

Building Self-Confidence

From the start of the camp, we work to foster attitudes that will not only encourage the campers to make the most of their three-week experience but also allow them to carry that experience into their daily lives when they return home. The return home, it should be emphasized, can be especially hard on the teenagers. Many of them become victims of scorn back home, and it requires considerable effort by our Jerusalem office staff to support them. Officials, friends, and even families often belittle the youngsters when they return, trying to shortchange their accomplishments. After returning home from Seeds of Peace, one Israeli girl explained that her classmates not only rebuked her efforts, but "they said stuff like 'You bitch! I can't believe you did that! You're a traitor! How could you meet with them? They're killing us.'" Amgad, an Egyptian boy, had a similar experience when he returned home. He wrote back to us, "Every day I'm bombarded, pressured into hating these people by others. I've been called a 'traitor' by many people, by my friends and some people I meet in the street."

To prepare our youngsters for this, we try to create an environment at camp that will engender a sense of self-confidence. From day one, the youngsters are told how important they are. They are told that they made it through a highly competitive selection process. They are told that the eyes of the world are on them. They are told that though government action is important, they are the ones who really matter in the end. And we don't just tell them. They live it. Journalists are often to be seen roaming around the camp, videotaping, snapping pictures, and asking the youngsters about their lives. The campers meet with diplomats in Washington. By the end of the program, many of them are convinced they are indeed important. One camper began the summer asking what all "the silly fuss" was about. He had never heard of Seeds of Peace in Israel. "It's nothing. It's not a big program," he told his counselor. By the end of the three weeks, he spent his nights demanding to know why Seeds of Peace was not more important in Israel and began planning how to publicize it at home.

Every year we invite about one-fifth of the prior year's campers to return as "program leaders." These former graduates act as role models for the new campers. As the younger campers watch the program leaders treat one another with respect and, more important, as close friends, they aspire to be in a similar situation. Many campers even emulate the program leaders' behavior because they hope that they too will be able to return to camp. Many of the campers, in moments of confusion, grow frustrated with themselves, their peers, and the process and consider withdrawing emotionally from the program; at such times, a program leader—a big brother or big sister figure from their own country—can pull them aside and make sure they stay involved with the camp program.

Part of building their self-confidence is acknowledging their accomplishments. As with any teenagers, their proudest moments are the times they are allowed to shine. We try to create as many of those moments as we can both at the camp and when they travel to Washington, D.C. The visit to the nation's capital provides an opportunity for interacting with members of Congress; for a tour of the National Space Museum, the Holocaust Museum, and other sites; and for a meeting or "photo-op" with the president, vice president, or secretary of state. This final salute to the youngsters helps reinforce their sense of mission. It allows them to return home believing in their accomplishments and certain that the adult world is paying attention.

No opportunity is missed to make them feel special. During the daily lineup, campers who have learned to swim or play tennis or who have written a poem are singled out and cheered. Their poems are read aloud. When they travel to the State Department or the White House, they eagerly compete with each other to speak publicly about their experience. Asked what her favorite moment was, Bushra said, "When I had a speech in 1995 at Harvard University and when I was in Washington and read my poem." After Ihab, a Palestinian, batted the ball to the outfield, he became noticeably more confident and open. Another Palestinian said the high point for her was simply playing soccer on the same team as Israelis. Yet another said that when an Israeli passed him the ball so that he could score on an Israeli goalkeeper, that was "unimaginable."

Such confidence can have untold effects. Sherif, an Egyptian, told a counselor that he had finally learned how to hug. "Now, I really will start changing my underwear," he announced.

Usually, the youngsters are asked to take on more productive challenges. In drama the youngsters are asked to improvise by exchanging roles, to become a mirror for the other, Palestinian to Israeli, or to write a scene together. On the ropes course, a possible life-and-death situation, the campers must trust one another to hold them up. What seem like tiny victories can add up in a camper's mind. If she can accomplish a small thing with her friend, then perhaps she can accomplish other small things, such as a polite political discussion or an honest question-and-answer session.

Their proudest accomplishments are often the simplest. "Picture this: an Israeli kid, a Palestinian kid, an Egyptian kid, and a Jordanian kid sleep next to each other, share their food, the soap, the toothpaste, everything. Tell me—is this a dream or reality?" asked Dan, an Israeli. "If you think it's a dream," he announced, "come to my bunk and see!" Seeds of Peace, notes Walzer, creates "a safe place for these kids where suddenly they can accept the enemy as a friend, as a brother, as a cohabitator. For Dan, the big accomplishment was not that he had accepted the Palestinian right to a state, but just coexistence in the most literal sense of the word. He is coexisting with Palestinians and he is proud of it. It means something to him. He is going to go home and tell his friends."

Floor hockey

Thinking and Speaking for Themselves

Once they begin to gain confidence in themselves, the campers are encouraged to go beyond that, to play a more public role, to speak out, to become spokespersons for what they are trying to achieve. Other bridge-building programs between hostile or adversarial groups insist on shunning the press, conducting their activities behind closed doors. We invite the media to visit and report on the camp, from the initial flag-raising ceremony, which is broadcast on the evening news on all three network affiliates in Maine, to the last day of camp, when the campers depart for Washington, D.C., en route home. This coverage helps validate for the youngsters that what they are doing is indeed important and newsworthy. It reminds them that they are part of the adult world, yet at the same time they are doing things the adults, their leaders, have not been able to do. Once they recognize this, they can begin to believe that they really will make a difference. After all, the world is paying attention to them. To buttress that, announcements are made each morning about the results of the coverage, and the clippings are posted in front of the dining hall. When they see their picture in the paper, they feel good about themselves. They see that there are rewards for the risks they are taking.

Often those risks, and rewards, are important in their development. Each camper soon realizes that he or she is responsible for what he or she says and thinks. In August 1993, before anyone knew about the secret negotiations being held between Israel and the PLO in Oslo, Norway, ABC-TV's "Good Morning America" sent a crew to Otisfield to do a "live" segment from the shores of the lake. It was the fourth day of our first summer. Two Israelis and two Palestinians were chosen for the interview. Neither of them had any idea of what they would be asked. During the interview, one of the Israelis took a hard line against the creation of a Palestinian state. But Yehoyoda, the other Israeli, said, "I think the Palestinians should have their own land." Afterward, he was proud of what he had said. But this concept, that Palestinians deserved a state, contradicted his government's position. When reports arrived later that day about what "Yoyo" had said, the Israeli delegation leader berated him. He even called him a traitor. "When I found Yoyo he had been crying for a couple of hours," recalled Barbara Gottschalk. "I asked him to stand up. I took him by two arms and held him tight, and I said, 'Yoyo, don't you ever let anyone else tell you what to say. If you had said the opposite of what you said, it would have been all right with us. It doesn't matter to us what you said. What is important is that you said what was in your mind and in your heart.'" That was a major turning point for him. He told his delegation leader that he would not retreat, that he was sorry if it had caused embarrassment but he believed in what he had said. Two days later, news of the secret Oslo talks became public. The networks reported that there were plans for Israel's prime minister, Yitzhak Rabin, and the PLO's chairman, Yasser Arafat, to meet. They would, the reports said, sign a document that could lead to eventual statehood for the Palestinians. "See, my government agrees with me," declared Yoyo. His courage to think and speak for himself had paid off.

Of course, the presence of camera crews can also inhibit youngsters from speaking candidly with one another. They may say what they think the cameras want to hear, and not what they really believe. But there also are situations where being suddenly thrust into the spotlight helps focus their thoughts. Often campers discover that they have ideas they were not even aware of.

Sometimes the media help to remind us of exactly why Seeds of Peace was founded. After a bus bombing in Jerusalem, the *Portland Herald*, the largest newspaper in Maine, carried a particularly gruesome photograph of Israeli corpses on its front page. The picture also showed an Orthodox rabbi comforting a badly wounded survivor. But beneath the fold, on the same page, there was a photo of Israeli and Palestinian teenagers holding hands. The story began: "Nowhere in this country was news of the savage and deadly bombing in West Jerusalem more heartfelt than in Otisfield." The photo and the article let the youngsters see for themselves that they were providing hope to a hope-starved world.

The campers are trusted to speak their minds publicly—forcing them to reflect on their experiences for themselves and to choose for themselves what is most valuable to impart. With no censorship from the staff and no threats of punishment for speaking "out of line," the campers know they have the full trust and faith of Seeds of Peace. They are not pawns to be moved around in the name of peace; they are the peacemakers themselves. This is clear from the profound and poignant questions they ask when they are introduced to prominent political figures such as the U.S. secretary of state. Believing in their own sense of importance and their own mission, they pepper leaders with questions that speak to their frustrations, hoping for answers that could actually help them move forward in their work. For years parents have told their children to be seen and not heard. At Seeds of Peace they are encouraged to jump up and scream, but to think for themselves while they do this, and they respond.

Maintaining Neutrality, Validating Identities

Remaining neutral is fundamental to the program. We do not espouse particular political solutions to the Arab-Israeli conflict, nor do we condemn others. Each youngster must come to his or her own understanding of the possibilities of peace. If we were to stake out our own political territory we would not only limit the range of those possibilities but also risk alienating youngsters who entered the program with fixed political beliefs. We cannot afford such alienation. Seeds of Peace offers youngsters the opportunity to come to their own resolution about the conflict; and it supports their efforts, and the efforts of their national political leaders, to deal peacefully and honestly with the "other side." In support of peace, however, we do not back down from condemning violence. We condemn outright the killing of innocent victims. And we condemn outright any violations of peace agreements both sides have signed.

We also go to great lengths to ensure that the students feel equal and equally validated. On the first morning after the youngsters' arrival, the flag of each participating nation is raised in front of the camp entrance. The large iron gates are closed behind them as all the youngsters and adults assemble for the opening ceremony. In alphabetical order, Egyptians, Israelis, Jordanians, Moroccans, Palestinians, Qataris, Tunisians, and Yemenis, and then Americans step forward, facing the rest of the group, to sing their national anthem while their flag is slowly raised. (The Israeli flag is positioned between the Jordanian and Palestinian flags to reflect their geographical position as neighbors.)

We want each camper to feel secure in, and proud of, his or her national identity. The strength that the campers derive from their separate identities ultimately allows them to bond in a community that spans national, political, and religious boundaries. Were Seeds of Peace not to raise flags or to sing anthems and simply ban the display of flags within the camp-ground, many youngsters would feel it necessary to assert constantly their national identity within the camp. But by standing at attention and focusing on campers from other countries as they raise their flags and sing their national anthems with gusto and pride, we convey a powerful message of respect for each camper's national identity. When they see that what they are fighting for is being expressed and accorded respect right from the start, the campers can move forward. Thereafter, they can concentrate on listening to one another instead of validating themselves. When the entire group cheers each delegation as it concludes its anthem, the first step is taken toward mutual recognition and acceptance.

This is not, however, always an easy time for the campers—especially the Arab Israeli campers, many of whom do not know which anthem to sing, the Palestinian or the Israeli. They are forced to make an immediate choice: do they, as citizens of Israel, stand with Jewish Israelis in front of their fellow Palestinians, singing the words of a song that they have been singing since they were children but that may make their Arab friends wince? Or do they sing with the Palestinians? Can they feel comfortable singing both? The campers do not always make it easy for one another. One Arab Israeli camper said that when she started to walk up and sing with the Israelis, her friend muttered "traitor" under her breath. The girl stopped at the crowd's edge and chose not to sing. An Israeli camper said she was proud that she had clapped after the Palestinian anthem, that this was an achievement for her, but said that later she "found out" that the anthem spoke against the Israelis, and she was ashamed.

Such a momentous and confusing event at the beginning of the program is a difficult one for the campers to deal with (it is often a subject that comes up later in the coexistence discussions). When we remember that these are just songs, we can begin to understand the complexities that these youngsters are forced to deal with. Seeds of Peace is unable to effect changes or eliminate these complexities. They are contextual realities of the Middle East. The struggle for an Arab Israeli to understand his or her loyalties is a unique one for each youngster, and we do not prescribe simple solutions to evade the issue. But we do insist on raising the flags. No matter what your stance, at Seeds of Peace everyone respects the status of all other peoples.

John Wallach leads a new nation of Seeds of Peace into camp after the flag-raising ceremony

Before each flag is raised, a program leader from each delegation speaks of his or her previous experience and what he or she has learned at Seeds of Peace. Each delegation listens carefully and applauds wildly for its youthful leader. After the flags are raised, the Seeds of Peace flag is raised and everyone sings the Seeds of Peace anthem, usually with arms around one another and often swaying to the rhythm. Then we march back through the giant iron gates and into the camp as one. We are all wearing the same T-shirts, and the occasion feels historic. We are leaving the flags and symbols outside and creating our own nation. This nation is governed not by hate and conflict, prejudice or ideology, but by the social norms that bring about honest trusting relationships and discussions. Some of the campers immediately recognize this and later speak of walking through the gates as one of their proudest moments.

The Seeds of Peace anthem (composed by James Durst, a folksinger, from a poem written by Amgad, an Egyptian camper)

People of Peace, rejoice, rejoice
For we have united into one voice;
A voice of peace and hate of war,
United hands have built a bridge between two shores.
We on the shores have torn down the wall,
We stand hand in hand as we watch the bricks fall.
We've learned from the past and fear not what's ahead;
I know I'll not walk alone,
But with a friend instead.

Chorus:
I am a Seed of Peace, seed of peace, a seed of peace
I am a seed, a seed of peace
I am a seed, I am a seed of peace
(Quietly) **Peace, Peace, Peace, Peace.**

Over the next three weeks, even more campers develop a sense of pride. As the following chapters describe, eventually we do seem to become a giant team: group cheers in the dining hall grow louder and louder; the youngsters begin to congregate in mixed groups more frequently; at public events, such as a night out at a baseball game, they cheer not only for the teams playing but for themselves, shouting during every inning for "Seeds of Peace ya da rat tat too!" The final meals are filled with group cheers to the point where you can barely eat. Coexistence becomes not the absence of war, but something to be proud of, something good, interesting, and fun. The youngsters develop a sense that peace, as well as dominance, can bear fruits. Peace is something worth taking pride in, something worth fighting for.

Living Together

Breaking the Stereotypes

One of my girls at the dinner table, she was very honest and she said that she'd be friends with a Jew, but it's in her blood she can never trust one. And I didn't understand. "Well you have to go there. It's just so deep," she said. "I'll never be able to trust them."

—SEEDS OF PEACE COUNSELOR, 1998

Growing Up with Stereotypes

Creating a community, however helpful, is not enough to change the youngsters' outlooks on the conflict or even on one another. Many of our youngsters know little about the history of the other side. Often, they know simply to blame them for the suffering of the present.

"Before I went to the Seeds of Peace camp, my idea about Israelis is just that they are soldiers, without any people. I didn't think that there are families with children and relatives—just soldiers with a gun, with a weapon. And I thought that all the Israelis, they hate Palestinians," said Bushra, who lives in the Al Aroub refugee camp near Hebron.

The stereotypes they have of one another often seem to be a product of their own experience. "Every day was a frightened day of my life, like every day because the intifada, the Palestinian uprising against Israeli rule, started in 1987 when I was six years old. That was my first time in school, my first year," explained Abdelsalam from Nablus, a Palestinian city in the West Bank. "Every day when we came home from school there was a soldier. There was throwing stones. And you know, a boy six years old, he will be very afraid of that. The picture of the Israelis in his mind will be very bad because of that. And you know, a lot of my friends were put in jail. I had one friend—he was killed by the soldiers. He was nine years old."

Lidor, an Israeli, confided that in his school the word "Arab" carries a particular stigma. "It is like a curse in slang Hebrew. When somebody plays some sport badly, the other ones say, you play like an 'Arab.' Or if someone is dressed ugly or eats improperly, 'Arab' is the word to describe him. The word 'Arab' means like 'primitive' in Hebrew slang."

Textbooks also fuel the stereotypes with which our youngsters arrive at camp. "When I used to speak about Arabs, it was from [what I had read] in Israeli books about Israeli history," said Roy, now a third-year program leader. "They picture Arab people as like Neanderthals, like the women are here and the men are there, and the men drag the women by the hair and stuff."

One Palestinian schoolbook says that Jews will abandon their deceitful ways only "when donkeys stop braying and serpents stop biting." According to another textbook, Jews "are haughty when they feel safe; they kill when they are able; and when they are afraid, they remind others of lofty morals so that they alone can benefit."

Even after the signing of a peace treaty between Israel and Jordan in 1995, our Jordanian campers told us about high schools where it is taught that any accord between Muslims and Jews is temporary until "God's destiny" destroys Israel. In one Egyptian school, children are taught that all Jews "hate Islam" and that "their lives are based on betrayal and treachery."

There also are Israeli textbooks that demean the Arabs. A second-grade text says that the first Zionists, the European Jews who immigrated to Palestine in the early 1900s, described the land as being "deserted and empty with only Turks and lazy Arabs sitting in it." Other Israeli history books ignore the presence of the half million Arabs who owned land and were citizens of the Ottoman Empire and the British Mandate of Palestine. Theirs is the story of heroic Jewish defenders, "strong as lions" who have the "light of eagles," fighting off hordes of fanatic Arab invaders.

Some textbooks also have a tendency to skip lightly over historical events that might encourage sympathy for the "other side" (in fact, we find that discussions at camp often fill in important gaps in knowledge that keep the youngsters from understanding one another's histories). For example, in the schoolbooks of Arab countries, the Holocaust, if mentioned, is often trivialized—one book describes it as "a Jewish excuse for a state." Some of the Arab youngsters come believing that the Holocaust was the Jews' own fault. "Jews shrank from confronting those who had committed them to the slaughterhouses and took retribution upon Palestinians in the scandalous horrifying manner which is endorsed by the West," reads an Islamic text used in religious instruction in Jordan.

Israeli youngsters are seldom taught about *al-Nakba*, the Arabic name for the "catastrophe" of the 1948 war, which forced hundreds of thousands of Palestinians from their homes when the state of Israel was born. And just as Jews are depicted in some Arab textbooks as having stolen the land from the Arabs, Israelis often are taught that the Palestinians who live in ancient Judea and Samaria (the parts of the West Bank where Abraham lived) have no right to be there at all. "The Promised Land will never be sold permanently because it belongs to God. Therefore you will hold onto all The Land for redemption," reads a textbook used in an Israeli settlement in Ofra.

Simply allowing the youngsters to coexist and form a community does not address these underlying attitudes and information. It would be easy for us, on the first or second day of camp, to sit the youngsters down and present them with a brief "objective" history of the conflict. We do not do that. Beyond the inherent danger of presenting a story that seems more biased to one side than to the other, there is the possibility that the students will simply tune it out or fight it. Instead, we allow the youngsters to explain to one another the history of the conflict as they see it, through their eyes and past experiences. But even this is not always enough. We have discovered that a change in attitudes requires a relationship between Arab and Israeli youngsters. The strongest way to break down these stereotypes is through personal relationships. So we insist that the youngsters "make one friend."

Making One Friend

It seems an odd mantra for a peace camp full of fearful and estranged teenagers, but "make one friend" is repeated time and again. As long as their relationships are primarily with members of their own delegation, the campers may never have the opportunity to see through the stereotypes they came with. And they will not develop the personal trust that allows for successful discussion. So we encourage them every day to make one real friend—someone with whom they can share their own stories, a friend they will want to see when they go home, unless parents and politicians stand in their way. At first the campers laugh at the challenge. After the first week they say they have made three, four, five, or a whole bunch of friends. But as they go through the program they discover how difficult making friends can be. The constant reminder keeps them focused on the reason they came in the first place.

"The first week, everybody did the same. The Israeli delegation was staying together and we were doing the same thing, the Palestinian delegation," recalls Hiba.

But I knew I went to the camp to make Israeli friends, and John Wallach, he was saying all the time "make one real friend." Then I said okay, I don't want to spend all this time with the Palestinian delegation because I will see them, I will talk with them. I can talk with the Egyptians, the Jordanians, but the Israeli . . . I must take my chances to talk with an Israeli. So we started to break the wall between us. We had many problems after the coexistence sessions. But I said to my friends, okay just forget the coexistence sessions, let's talk about ourselves. It's very nice when you tell a friend, okay, I'm Hiba, I play basketball, I like this thing and that thing. You feel closer to each other. That's what happened. We started talking about ourselves and we became friends.

Nancy, an Egyptian girl, said she never dreamed she would "pray with Israelis before I go to sleep, eat from the same main dish three times a day, and share our differences. In fact, our differences have brought us closer together."

Friendships can start from different experiences, or experiences together. Tomer, an Israeli, said that before he played soccer with them he had never been aware of his prejudice toward Palestinians. There were only three good players on his team, he said. When one of them got hurt and had to leave the game, Tomer and the other player had to carry the ball.

They had like three or four guys and we were down by a goal. They got another goal and our morale was low. We lost the game 4–2 or 5–2, something really embarrassing, but I remember the way we played together, and the way we [Tomer and the other player] comforted each other after we lost. It was a very good feeling for me. One of my biggest amazements was that I never knew that he was Palestinian. I was sure he was Egyptian. I never realized that I treated them differently. It was something in my subconscious. Then I realized that I cannot tell who is Egyptian and who is Palestinian. I never told that to anyone but I was ashamed that before that I had made a distinction between them. I have never done it again. It was a big lesson that I learned.

Through simply playing soccer, Tomer had broken through levels of prejudice and alienation. For many, realizing the fact of their own friendships is a moving experience. As one facilitator explained:

> Some of this stuff I get really choked up about. We were talking in our session about images of the other, images of the enemy. Visual images and verbal images and we talked about what do you think of when you think of the enemy? A lot of them said, "You know, I always thought of Israelis, I thought of guns, I thought of soldiers being brutal and what have you." And Sara spoke up with tears in her eyes and her voice choked and she said, "I wish"—she pointed to a Tal, an Israeli girl across the room—and she said, "She is my friend and I wish you could have seen us yesterday. We were playing ping-pong and it was beautiful." Those were her words; they are forever in my mind. The act of playing ping-pong; it was beautiful to her because before coming here she never in her lifetime imagined herself playing ping-pong with an Israeli.

These simple friendships can blossom, becoming the key to repairing strained political relationships. One Israeli girl wrote to us later:

> There were pictures there, pictures of a Palestinian mother mourning at her son's death and a picture of a group of Israelis mourning at their friend's death. . . . We didn't know what to say. . . . Dina, an Egyptian girl, started crying and went outside. After coexistence was over we had to go to sailing. I chose to go with Dina. I thought maybe a conversation with her may calm her down. We went on the sailing boat and then we started laughing, over nothing. . . . all of a sudden we started laughing. We started talking and we made a rule that we won't talk about politics once the coexistence was over. Seeing her smile made me feel very good. . . . When we reached shore, I went with Dina to her bunk. She told me that she was very emotional today because she didn't expect to see those pictures. . . . she then showed me her family's pictures and told me a story about her uncle's death at the Yom Kippur War. I realized that coexistence starts with those small things.

Dina might never have opened herself up without the friendship of this young Israeli. And the Israeli would never have seen the suffering of Dina's family.

Dana, an Israeli girl, tells a similar story about her experience at camp during the bombing by the Palestinian organization Hamas on Ben Yehuda Street in Tel Aviv in the summer of 1997:

> I didn't know who I was that day, who I was hugging. I was just there and they were there. I know that the Palestinians were there more than anybody. The

Israelis were there and they were sharing my pain and they couldn't talk [about] it and I couldn't talk to them and they couldn't comfort me. So I found comfort more with the Palestinians than the Israelis. I never thought a Palestinian could comfort me over what a Palestinian did.

When your enemy pays attention to you, has fun with you, comforts you, it is a tremendous event. Your enemy has done something for you—anything is possible.

An Israeli girl leans on her Palestinian friend for comfort

Coexistence Sessions

Owning Up and Reaching Out

Dear Diary, today at Facilitation group the Palestinians and the Israelis had a fight. We always fight with the Palestinians.... Sometimes I think we all feel lost between all the screams. The facilitators try to calm us down—sometimes I think they're even shocked that we get to topics like Jerusalem by just mentioning where we live. I scream too, and it seems like no one listens.... Aviv keeps talking about the Israeli army, I talk about Jerusalem, Fidaa talks about Palestinian refugees, Karen speaks facts, their facts.... Ayala and I are always in eye contact as if we plan what we want to say. Today our biggest fight was about Israel and a Palestinian state. It became a fight about a refugees' camp, which turned into a fight about Jerusalem, don't ask how.

—An Israeli Seed of Peace, July 1998

For two hours each day, led by a pair of facilitators, groups of twelve campers participate in discussions we call "coexistence sessions." It is the youngsters' daily place to be honest and frank, to express their reactions to camp and to one another. It doesn't take long for their real feelings to emerge. So it is here that we must look to understand the deeper layers of change that the youngsters are able to achieve.

Coexistence sessions are a messy, emotional experience. The youngsters speak of their suffering, their frustrations, and their vision for the future. They argue about politics and prejudice. For weeks they circle from argument to argument, often surfing through angry tirades. On some nights, through the window of a cabin, you can see ten or twelve youngsters all with heads down, sobbing together, each immersed in his or her own pain. On other nights a student runs out of the coexistence session in anger, or twenty minutes of pure shouting go by—what one youngster called "our new sound-based weaponry." Below the surface lie incredible hatreds. To build an honest peace, the youngsters have to deal with them.

The sessions are a mix of nationalities—four Israelis, four Palestinians, and four other youngsters either from the Arab countries or the United States. The first days are easygoing, as at camp on the whole; facilitators must establish a safe and supportive environment, and they use the time to do so. But soon the facilitators delve into what is on the youngsters' minds. The experience at camp can be enough to start a discussion rife with emotion. The facilitators are not just looking for argument. They are looking to explore the youngsters' thoughts about one another—to lay bare the points of conflict so that the youngsters can find solutions.

This isn't easy. The campers are not prepared to simply explain to one another the origin of their stereotypes (if they are aware of them) or their most embarrassing prejudices. They are not ready to share the ways they have been hurt or the indignities they have suffered. The facilitators use a range of approaches. A team from New York City role-plays a racial conflict and allows the youngsters to express themselves through empathizing and coaching the characters onstage. A Palestinian and Israeli team use highly emotional photographs to spark similar discussions of empathy and personal exploration. One facilitator simply asks about the students' own anxieties of being at camp, allowing the mix of fear, guilt, or pride in their own actions to become an entranceway into exploring the emotions the youngsters have toward each other. Another facilitator asks the students to draw the mosaic of their lives and then lets the instinct to share their feelings take over as they explain each drawing they have included.

Below the Smile: Surfacing Anger

It doesn't take long for the youngsters to realize they don't like what they hear. There are not only myths and stereotypes, but two sets of facts to the conflict. Hearing the new stories immediately challenges the youngsters. Early on they often spend time straightening out myths and poor facts—a fundamental movement within the coexistence sessions. As the youngsters move from discussion to argument, no matter the topic, a base of secure knowledge grows. This is especially apparent if the youngsters really trust each other. Some of our older youngsters will go to certain friends for facts. When Laith, a Palestinian, struggled with the importance of the Holocaust, he finally threw up his hands and said, "Please, tell me, I want to hear it from Yoyo," an old Israeli friend.

But often questioning is like a test. The youngsters compare their own stereotypes with the real people before them. Many Israelis begin asking what the Palestinians think of the Holocaust, knowing full well that to the Palestinians the Holocaust is just an Israeli excuse for occupation. Palestinians will make a clear point of declaring that they are from "Palestine," a word that to Israelis is packed with implications of a return to the British Mandate, or in other words, the destruction of Israel. "Sometimes a Palestinian kid asked me where I'm from and he knew that I was from Israel, from Ashdod. 'Where is Ashdod?' he asked. 'In Israel,' I said. He said, 'No, in Palestine.'" It does not take long for the tone to move from questioning to confrontation.

The youngsters are quick to discover conflicting thought. "Okay, one of these girls had a necklace of Israel with a Palestinian flag on it [wearing any kind of political symbol is discouraged at Seeds of Peace], and she took it off, and I respect that, but she asked: Why can she not wear it? . . . I came to her and told her to listen. Fifty years ago, that might have been Palestine but we conquered it. Yes, we might have conquered it in different ways, we might have paid for the land, we might have occupied it, you might have even given us some of the parts, but the point is that now it's ours and we are proud of that."

The arguments run from fights over Jerusalem to issues of semantics. In the following example, Keren, an Israeli, and Ghadeer, a Palestinian, argue over the term "madman," jumping from there to a discussion of the Holocaust:

Keren:	People from the Holocaust did immigrate or run to other places before they came to Israel.
Ghadeer:	About the Holocaust, we have the same situation in Palestine.
Keren:	Don't compare, no, no, don't compare.
Palestinian (a):	When he [Baruch Goldstein, an Israeli settler who killed thirty Palestinians on February 25, 1994] entered the Ibrahim mosque, and he started to kill the prayers, the people praying, can you explain that?
Keren:	I can't explain, he was a madman.

Palestinian (b): Okay, how come every time that someone kills people, you are mad but . . .

Palestinian (a): It seems like you are giving your land to mad people. They might as well give it to proper people . . .

Palestinian (b): When you do something you are mad but when we do something we are terrorists!

Keren: People who go onto a bus and explode themselves are terrorists!

Negotiating Everything

As one youngster later explained, early discussion time is a period of verbal negotiation. When they hear something they know runs against their nation's position, they respond only with attacks.

> Everyone's goal was to prove himself right and to work to show that the other side was indeed behaving as expected, according to the stereotype associated with him. Only post facto did we understand that this was because the stereotype was our defense. The existence of a stereotypical image that we attributed to the Palestinians was our justification for the military policy that existed in the Territories [the West Bank and Gaza]. Changing the stereotype was tantamount to an admission that we had been wrong as a state and no one was prepared to admit that. The same attitude guided the other side. Only if they viewed us as a cruel conqueror were they able to find justification for killing and terrorism. Any departure from this labeling was tantamount to an admission that terrorism harmed innocent civilians and should be condemned.

The youngsters rarely listen to each other, instead using the time when others speak to prepare their own statements in their heads. They seemed fueled by their desire not to budge an inch, not to admit anything that would undermine their position.

Debate often revolves around challenging claims to the land. Justice becomes an argument against history. "Malak, you said that from your roots and generations ago, Palestine belonged to the Palestinians," said Adi, an Israeli. "What I'm saying is that according to our rules, according to our people, generations and generations ago, Palestine and Israel was ours. The Torah says it was ours. God gave that land to us."

Malak replied, "They should first of all give the [land] to the people who are already there, and were there hundreds of years ago, before they accept other people who just came last year or who did not stay there and see the land getting built."

"How do you know that the people in Israel are not the ancestors of these ancient Jews?" asked Adi.

"So why didn't you try to return to the Holy Land for thousands of years?" asked another Palestinian. "Obviously the Torah wasn't the boss." But "we did try. We did try," said Adi.

The youngsters spend most of their time looking for ways to deflate the comments of the other side. Instead of imagining how the speaker feels or seeking to understand where he or she is coming from, the youngsters begin thinking hard and fast of what they will say next. Their mind flips through a Rolodex of rebuttals, switching topics if needed, but never simply acknowledging the validity of what their "enemy" has to say. The youngsters come up with endless ways to avoid a simple "Wow, I didn't know that" or "Thank you for telling me that." The argument is spurred on by the youngsters themselves, as they refuse to yield on the smallest points as well as the biggest issues. And as they continue to fight, the youngsters become more and more embroiled in proving the righteousness of their own cause. In the following discussion including Roy, a second-year Israeli camper, the comments of Mohammed and two first-year Israelis show how clearly each side strives to prove its righteousness:

Roy: You say we need to get to a certain point of understanding. But I believe we got to a certain point because when Mohammed introduced me, he said that I'm from Israel. I know it's hard for Mohammed to say I'm from Israel because he believes the entire country is Palestine. He believes I'm from Palestine. But he got to a point where he understands that I'm from Israel so it shows a certain understanding of my beliefs. It felt kind of good, that someone listens to me, doesn't stay in his own opinion without considering my beliefs.

Mohammed: Do you believe in Palestine?

Roy: I believe that when Palestine will be [exist], then I will say there is a Palestine. But now Palestine is the Gaza Strip and part of the West Bank.

Israeli (a):   You mean Palestine is not yet a country just a territory.

Mohammed: I understand in the future but not now. Why not now?

Israeli (a):   Because it's part of Israel.

Mohammed: Do you know about UN Resolutions 242 and 338? [These resolutions, adopted by the United Nations Security Council after the Arab-Israeli wars of 1967 and 1973, essentially called for a settlement of the refugee problem, withdrawal of Israeli forces from "territories" occupied in 1967, and the independence of every state in the region within secure and recognizable borders.]

Israeli (a):   You invaded our lands.

Mohammed: We now have a flag, and lands, and a government, and an army.

Israeli (b):   This shows you are a country but not a real country. You don't have an ambassador to the United Nations. You don't have the important things like an army.

Roy: Let's decide what are the important things. They have a flag and an anthem and are related to the lands. That's the important thing, not side things you have when you have a country.

Israeli (b):   But they don't have any impact.

Facilitator: Are you saying Palestine is on its way to being a recognized country? Mohammed, do you hear that?

Mohammed: If you look at 242 and 338, we have the country now.

Israeli (b):   242 said the land is divided into Palestine and Israel. In 1948 we were happy with our part. You started the war. You started the war, not us.

Mohammed: How?

Israeli (b):   You attacked the country.

Facilitator: You say "you" and "us." What are you saying when you say "you"? Do you realize when you say "you" you are talking to Mohammed? He didn't start the war in '48.

Israeli (b):   I understand. Mohammed wasn't born in '48.

Facilitator: [to Mohammed] Do you also understand? What's the difference between representing your country and representing yourself?

Israeli (b):   Sometimes it's very difficult. If I am here as a representative of a country, I don't need to attack the decisions.

Mohammed: I mean when I said you are from Israel, I meant the occupation inside Palestine called Israel. Do you understand me? The occupation inside Palestine called Israel.

Roy: A lot of Palestinians don't believe there is Israel at all. A lot.

Mohammed: We believe occupation, that you occupied our land Palestine. You are an occupying country, not a country like Egypt. You are an occupying country.

Facilitator: You are saying you recognize Israel but you recognize it as occupied Palestine?

Mohammed: I'm saying inside Palestine there is the occupation called Israel.

Israeli (b):   Do you understand that in the peace process the Israeli people recognized Palestine and the Palestinian people recognized Israel? If you don't recognize Israel, what is it all for, the peace process?

Israeli (a):	He is saying there is no Israel, that we don't have a country.
Roy:	He's saying we are part of your country.
Israeli (b):	At this time there is no Palestine. You're not talking here about facts. You're talking about opinions. I know it's hard to say it but it's the truth.
Mohammed:	When I said he's [Roy] "from Israel," we believe that the occupation inside Palestine is called Israel. It's not my opinion. We believe this.
Facilitator:	Do you believe Israel is a country?
Mohammed:	Occupation.
Facilitator:	Do you believe Palestine is a country?
Mohammed:	[laughing] Of course. It's not just my opinion. Other people too.
Israeli (b):	I'm asking you if you know that fact [that Israel exists]? This is what is important here because I have opinions too. But this is the fact. Your leader signed in the peace process that Israel is a country and that the Palestinians recognize this country. Do you support this peace process or not? Yes or no? Simple question.
Mohammed:	We now have a kind of country and you have an "occupation" country. When we will have our country, a "country" country, not like what we have now, you will have a country if you fulfill the agreement, not just a few of the agreements, and forget some.
Israeli (b):	We could say the same thing about you. Yes or no? After that, you can explain yourself as you wish.
Mohammed:	You now have an occupation country. If you'll carry out the agreements, you'll have your country as a country and we'll have our country as a country. You'll have yours and we'll have ours.

Recognizing the Difficulty

As argument follows argument, the youngsters are filled with frustration at what the other side says, and yet confused by the simple humanity of the people they see before them. Some react in pure dejection and demand to go home (no one has ever actually left). Filled with shame over their mixed emotions, others become very angry at themselves or at their compatriots. They call friends from their own delegations "traitors." "I feel they want to talk," explained one facilitator. "They want to make peace. But they feel confusion. They are in great confusion, and they are full of anger because they have this stereotype. They have their background and now they want to change many things. But they are influenced by their history books, by their teachers."

They want to make peace, but they are beginning to sense the difficulty. Upon hearing things she did not like, Keren, an Israeli youngster, decided she would be just as glad to withdraw and go home. She had heard Palestinians attack her and her country. She said she had come to Seeds of Peace to "make peace." Now that she understood what was involved, she said she was not sure she was still "with peace" at all.

Tomer, an Israeli, put it from his perspective: "I had a mid-camp crisis. I knew nothing I could say would help those who didn't understand. Nothing I could say would help them." It is the task of Seeds of Peace to help the campers through this difficult period, to reassure them that their loss of hope (and willpower) is natural, that now they may be able to understand how difficult it is to "make peace" and why it has been so hard for their leaders. Nevertheless, as one youngster explained, "it sometimes frustrates you that, really, you're talking to a wall."

From Frustration to Empowerment

For those who carry a great deal of pain, simply speaking about their righteousness can be incredibly important. As they face the wall of their enemy, these youngsters offer an endless array of not only defensive remarks, but often hurtful ones. Noa, an Israeli, recalled one time a Palestinian in her workshop said Israel had neither culture nor history. "That really hurt me," she explained, "because these are the things that define who I am."

They may also go to extraordinary extremes to deny the pain expressed from the other side. Some of the youngsters simply remain silent and won't comment when others speak. Some resort to parroting their government's positions, proclaiming that they are here only to represent their leaders. More often, students will look for more powerful ways of rejecting their enemy's statements, including blaming the other side's pain on the other side itself. This is an exchange between Mohammed, a Palestinian, and Zachi, an Israeli:

Mohammed:	How can I sleep in my house when the settlement is near my home and I hear soldiers all night, all the time, walking near my home and killing Palestinian people?
Zachi:	Oh, so it's all night, all night, every night, all night long they are just walking in the streets and looking for Palestinians to kill? That happens every day, every night?
Mohammed:	No, not every night.
Zachi:	I don't hear about a lot of Palestinians being killed.
Mohammed:	In the morning. In the afternoon. Even in the night.

Zachi:	I don't hear you saying that Palestinians get killed when they sit in their homes and are not throwing stones. In Hebron in the last four weeks, I think it was one or two men who got killed. You said that every day, every day in Gaza, there are a lot of killings.
Mohammed:	There are injuries too, lots of injuries.
Zachi:	With Israelis too; the soldiers are getting hurt too.
Mohammed:	But you have one soldier injured. We have twenty, twenty injured to your every one.
Zachi:	I'm not trying to compare suffering. You are trying to blame us for your pain, for your feeling unsafe. Look, where is the problem? In you, not in us, because you are responsible for your pain, not us. I mean you are the one that's throwing stones. Our soldiers are just protecting themselves.
Mohammed:	We throw stones because of what your government does, like taking land.
Zachi:	But there are other ways to express yourself.
Mohammed:	Excuse me, but you want to know why we throw stones? I want to help you. Ask me why, why am I throwing stones? Because I see my lands, our lands, Palestinian lands stolen every day, every day. I see my city destroyed and the building of settlements every day. I see my two friends killed. I see blood on the ground. I see my aunt die in an ambulance when soldiers, your soldiers, stopped the ambulance and talked with the driver. She died in the ambulance because the soldiers stopped the ambulance. I see children, a lot of children on the street. If you ask one of the children where is your father, he will tell you he is in prison in Israel or he is killed, killed by Israeli soldiers. How can I see all this . . .
Zachi:	Why is he in prison? What do you think? Do you think Israeli soldiers kill people? Why should Israeli soldiers kill people? I mean why? What can they gain from this? You said your aunt died in an ambulance? Where did the ambulance go? To an Israeli hospital?
Mohammed:	No.
Zachi:	Where?
Mohammed:	Inside the [Gaza] strip. Three checkpoints, four. [Apparently a terrorist attack had taken place earlier and a manhunt was under way for the perpetrators.] What could my aunt do? She wanted to give birth. But they stopped the ambulance.
Zachi:	A lot of times there were terrorists who are put in ambulances.
Facilitator:	Wait. Can you understand what he's saying? Did you just hear what he said?

Zachi:	Yes.
Facilitator:	How do you think Mohammed is feeling about that?
Zachi:	I understand his feeling. But he always wants to blame us. He needs to accept his part in the suffering of his people.

Abdelsalam, another Palestinian in the group, took an almost perverse pleasure in hurting Noa. "She was crying and I was very happy," recalled the Palestinian, "because I had made one Israeli cry. That was like a victory for me." Only later, he said, did he realize that "before she's an Israeli, she's a human. Before. And before I'm a Palestinian, I'm a human."

Hurting others can be an empowering experience. "Waffa, this Palestinian from Gaza, and Noa are in the same coexistence group," explained their bunk counselor. "Noa would come back to the bunk in tears. Waffa would come back so charged, so excited, so thrilled. The dichotomy between them was amazing. . . . I think for the Palestinians it's a very different thing. I think for her coming from Gaza, to be able to kind of scream at the Israeli is very empowering."

Marieke van Woerkom, a cultural anthropologist who helped chronicle the stories included in this book, saw a similar experience. "One of the girls came in tears, an Israeli girl. The Palestinian girl who was also in that session came kind of smiling, not quite, but from the same session, where she had been able to make herself be heard, probably for one of the first times. Whether people agreed or not, she was heard. It was empowering for her to see that Israeli upset. She had to feel like 'I said my thing, I finally had a chance to put it out there.'"

"For some of these kids, they don't really care that the other person totally agrees with them," noted Joachim, a counselor. It is important for them "just to be able to say this, to say it to the other side and to discover you are not alone in your opinion; maybe another Israeli or non-Israeli agrees with you and says, 'Yeah, I'm glad you said that.' Empowering, even if you don't change another person's opinion, is literally giving somebody a voice. A voice doesn't mean that you always get heard. In the adult world, we don't always get heard. But sometimes we simply need to speak."

This sense of empowerment is an important step for the youngsters. They are able to move beyond self-pity and come closer to acknowledging their own role in the conflict. They are forcing the people around them to understand their pain, even to experience it. Yet if the youngsters themselves don't re-experience the pain as well, if they simply force it onto other people, they are not able to make a connection between their suffering; they only re-affirm the righteousness of their cause. As long as they continue to pursue that argument, they remain closed to the other side. The youngsters are not accepting or acknowledging what those around them have to share.

Comparing Suffering: The Pain behind Hatred

If a student can truly come to understand the other side's suffering, he or she can understand a great deal about how to build a peaceful future. "Security" is not easily swallowed by Palestinians as an explanation for closures of Palestinian territory, though that is what Israeli politicians usually cite. Palestinian complaints that "the peace process is not fast enough" do not seem an understandable justification for taking pride in groups such as the Islamic fundamentalist organization Hamas, some of whose followers have engaged in suicide bombings and planted bombs on crowded Israeli streets. The fact that Hamas also supports Palestinian welfare centers and is generally regarded as less corrupt than the PLO is something Israeli teenagers learn from their Palestinian counterparts. In coexistence, the youngsters can really explain why they believe what they believe; they can explain why their people have taken action.

"The things that were happening were really bad," explained a Jordanian about the intifada:

> I'm not saying people from your side didn't get killed. And . . . there was just, there was a lot of killing, there was a lot of pain on their side and it was every day, it wasn't like one burst or anything like that, it was just people, it kept going on, every day you'd open the radio and you hear that someone in this city died, that two children got killed, or a mother was thrown off a cliff or something, and it's hard you know, it builds up, and then you just have to explode. It's just human nature, because you can't, you can't listen to it every day, you can't have your family being shot down all over the country. You can't have your brothers being shot down all over the country . . . even I, I was living in Jordan, every day I open the news and I hear that people are getting killed, I mean I want to do something about it, I want to bang my head against the wall or something. It just builds up. You have to do something, get on the street.

And yet the youngsters, at this stage, are barely listening. Instead they compare their suffering. "Well, you know, the bombs in Israel, many people are getting killed," the Israeli replied. "What about the families of Israeli people? Don't you think that they want revenge?"

"Hey, I live in fear every day. What do you think—going on a bus is easy?" asked Dana, another Israeli. "Going on a bus is so hard," she said. "A couple of months ago, one of my mom's friends got like 'boom,' blowed up and she didn't do anything. She wanted to give the Palestinians a country more than anybody in Israel but 'kaboom,' just like that. . . . Do you think I don't live in fear? Shit, I live in such fear," she said. That could be the doorway to a young Palestinian understanding that the Israeli fear is real and rational—if the youngster is ready to hear. Early on in the sessions the youngsters fight such talk. They refuse to put themselves in one another's shoes.

While the youngsters continue to reject the other side's comments, they remain locked into numerous other beliefs that fuel stereotypes and prejudice. If they believe that the enemy has not suffered or is to be blamed for its own suffering, they often believe that the enemy has chosen violence over peace for no good reason. They will begin to think the enemy is either aggressive or stupid. In this argument about plans in 1948 by the United Nations to partition the British Mandate of Palestine, we can see how a Palestinian's inability to see through Israeli eyes brings him to believe in instinctual Israeli aggression. Says one Israeli, "There would have been a little Palestine and a little Israel." Responds the Palestinian, "Where did you learn that, where? I have my own info and I don't think that your story is true." "So what's yours?" replied the Israeli. "I think that you came in and you just wanted all the win. . . . If you're starving, okay, and somebody gives you half a loaf of bread, wouldn't you take the whole thing? That's exactly what you did." The arguments continue without end. At every turn, the youngsters find a way to challenge the righteousness of their enemy's cause.

It is clear that as they argue, the youngsters' sense of suffering is so great that they feel a tremendous pressure to prove it should not have happened. Time after time, the same simple question is raised: Should this have happened to me?

"You came to a land. You called it Israel. You put yourself a government," explained a Palestinian youngster.

> You have your flag, your national anthem, and everything. I know it's in your Torah but it's not right now because we have different facts. You can't say, "But it's our land" because it's also our land, and what we're saying is that before the immigration into Israel by Jews from all over the world, is it fair that people who have been living there, who are Palestinian, who are Arabs, can be displaced by Israel, by Jews coming from all over the world, who have never been there before? You're displacing Arabs who have lived there, who have planted trees on soil they believe to be theirs, and is supposed to be theirs because their parents were there, their grandparents were there, and their great-grandparents were there. Is it fair to come to an Arab's house, a Palestinian house, and the land he planted with the sweat of his brow, and take him out of his house? He is now homeless. You put a Jew in his place who has just arrived fresh off the plane. Is that fair?

The obvious answer is that of course this isn't "fair," such suffering should not take place, but the other youngsters will rarely allow themselves such thoughts. Caught in the desire to prove their suffering unjust, the youngsters fire back only retorts in kind. Here, an Israeli speaks of giving up settlements, settlements she has probably never visited. "Wait, I'm gonna ask you, before they returned Gaza, people were living there, right? People were living there, they lived there all their lives, they have, they built there. Is it fair to take them out of their place because we have to give them to the Arabs to make peace? Is that fair? How do you think they feel?"

As they return again and again to the topic of who has suffered more, it becomes clear that the youngsters badly need to speak of their own pain; they are pushing for the discussion to turn to *their* stories. When they blame the other side for their problems, they are suggesting that the "real" cause of the cycle rests in the injustice done to *them*. As one facilitator puts it, "You use the word 'discuss.' I don't think in my opinion what is going on is discussing. It's a ventilation: 'I suffer more, I have more pain than you.' . . . And the question has to be now, 'So what?' . . . But they still are not at that stage. It's still the stage of 'look what you did to me, look what you did to me.'"

Self-Regulation: Ending the Argument

Often, usually at some point during the second week, the youngsters feel as though they can fight no more. They are sick of it. They have now learned the intellectual part of their lesson—they can see that each side has its story to tell. Truly connecting to that story will come later. For now at least, they have begun to acknowledge its existence.

"I think that both of you are totally right," said one Israeli bystander in a coexistence argument. "But the thing is, history happened and we can't change it, and both of us, Israelis and Arabs, have facts. And the facts that we might have might be different and might be the same, but it's facts and I don't think that either one of us is going to change his facts because it's true in both cases. Both of us have different facts and to keep fighting about it will lead nowhere."

An Arab youngster agrees: "All the points, it was clear about the past. I mean they had their own opinions and we had our own opinions on what happened. They had their story and we have a lot of—we have completely different opinions about the past and of course we can't forget about it, but there's other things that we need to talk about that are happening now, what's the problem that we are facing now, you know, in the present."

Sharing Tears, Finding the Connection

And yet as quickly as they dismiss the urge to talk about the past, the youngsters find themselves drawn back in. One student suggests forgetting the past, and another reminds them the past is why they are here. One student comments that they must focus only on the future, and another says he will not. "I never get sick of arguing," said one Israeli youngster. "I had two friends die in a terrorist bombing. I am here for them." The youngsters return to fighting and shouting until they have pushed themselves to an emotional edge. The edge is difficult; the youngsters are uncomfortable shouting at each other. But the real discomfort lies just below. They want to share why they are so upset. They want to explain what they have been through themselves, what their family has experienced. They want to explain that no matter what the other side says, what they have suffered should never happen to anyone. This is hard. To show or experience pain in front of others is embarrassing. To do so in front of the enemy is worse. It shows weakness. Such subjects are not spoken of.

The facilitators do what they can to let the youngsters open up. If the arguing is emotional enough, quick enough, the youngsters will open themselves in anger, expressing their outrage by reliving their own suffering. When these moments of sharing pain and hurt come to pass, the sessions can become tearful places. Sometimes the youngsters cry simply because they feel so pressured to prove their righteousness they feel unable to stand up to the burden. This is perhaps the closest they will ever come to sharing their suffering with someone else, or simply re-experiencing it. Facilitators may take this moment to ask them to share their thoughts, opening the door to sharing a story of pain. Often one youngster's tears will inspire another's. "I started to cry because I was very sad," explained one Palestinian youngster after seeing Israelis mourn the deaths caused by the Ben Yehuda bombing. "I saw the pain in their eyes, and I remembered things which happened in Palestine like [Israeli attacks on] Sabra and Shatila [in Lebanon] or the al-Aqsa mosque and Hebron. I remembered many things, not just the people killed in Jerusalem two days ago. I remembered many things and I started to cry." Such experiences are powerful for the youngsters. In re-experiencing their own pain, they legitimize its horror; in seeing such pain through their enemy, they begin to finally open up. They begin to see their connection.

When they do listen to each other's pain, it can have a powerful effect. Mohammed, a Palestinian, shared feelings close to his heart:

You were very angry about what I said yesterday and about the way in which I spoke, but this is my role which I learned from your soldiers in your government because your people taught me to be angry and because my heart is broken a lot of time and until now my heart is broken. So when I said that you are a country without a culture and without history it is because your government tried to burn my culture and my history. You are very angry when someone says that he is from Palestine, and you understand that he is from Jaffa or Haifa. I think you do that because you know that this land, which is also part of 1948 or 1967, is Palestine from the beginning of history.

About suffering you said that you suffered in bombings and you can't find safety in buses. I agree with you that you can't find safety in buses but I can't find it in my home or in my school or in my hospital. The only place I found safety is in the cemetery. What you said to me—you must forget the past—I answer that I must remind you about my past because I am afraid of what your government did to my uncle and my friend. I am afraid that they will do the same to me or my father. And I need to live in peace with my family, with my friends, and maybe with my sons and daughters and my wife. The most important thing that I will say is that I am not talking about my past to make your heart broken but you must listen to my past to understand my life and my story because you must know peace.

Noa said hearing Mohammed had been a new experience for her. "It was much more real to hear a personal story coming from feelings, very deep feelings. It made me feel, I was crying or about to cry, and I felt really sad. It was the way that it came from . . . he was talking from his heart, it wasn't politics talk. It was real pain, a real loss, and that meant much more and it really affected me more than if we were talking on the level of governments or as countries. We were talking like person to person like real people with feelings and that had a great impact on me."

Reliving their own sense of suffering allows the youngsters to put it behind them. The story of their pain is the most important thing they had to say. Once it has been shared, the youngsters no longer have a predetermined mission. They no longer have to prove the injustice of their past. One girl wrote in her diary:

Last night was strange. I don't think I could ever forget how Liron, Omer, Gil, and I went outside and how everyone started crying, and the silence in our bunk. I wanted to say something but I didn't know what to say. A day after, everyone sat and talked, no shouts. . . . Today there were no shouts, screams, yellings. Everyone listened—no exception! We even reached some agreements about a few subjects. At the end of the session, everyone had to say something good about each and every one of us. It was quite cool.

When they share their pain, openly and honestly with one another, there is very little left to fight about. The questions become, What does that pain mean to you? Should I be crying? Should my pain go on? When the youngsters see one another in pain they can answer the questions for themselves. When another's tears remind them of their own, they can begin to see that another's suffering is real.

Some need more than just seeing the other side in pain to feel relieved of their burden. Some youngsters need a sign that their enemy cares for them. They need to be listened to before they start listening on their own. As camp goes on and the friendships grow stronger, it becomes easier and easier for the youngsters to reach out in just this way.

"I got into a political argument with some of my Arab friends," recalled Noa, an Israeli:

> We were all saying things that the other side didn't really want to hear. So I asked a dear Palestinian friend of mine to take a walk with me. We sat down by the lake and the first thing that she said to me was, "You know, Noa, you are my friend and I love you and I care about you and that is why I am going to speak openly with you." In that moment I wanted to cry because I felt that I wanted to make a very big space for her inside my heart. I wanted to listen to what she had to say and I wanted to feel with her pain because I knew that she was doing the same thing for me. We talked a very long time and we reached out to each other as individual people with feelings and as friends.

Having heard that she was cared for, Noa left behind the worries about proving whether or not her experiences were unjust. She no longer felt the pressure to prove anything. Stanley Walzer tells a similar story:

> There is a very small Israeli boy in this camp named Eran who constantly picks on the small Arab boy in the next bed for speaking Arabic in the bunk. One day when I went into the bunk, Eran and the small Arab boy were fighting. I heard Eran yelling at him: "Hey you! Do not speak Arabic in this bunk!" Another Israeli boy, Yoachi, comes over and tries to settle the dispute. At that point, a tall Arab boy, Abal, walks into the bunk and, in Arabic, asks the small Arab boy: "What's going on here?" The small Arab boy snaps at him: "The problem is . . . like right now . . . we are talking Arabic—not English." Abal looks at him, very angrily and says, "Don't you ever correct me in front of an Israeli. You talk to me outside alone, outside. Now get outside."
>
> Eran seemed to miss this and again starts yelling at the young Arab boy. I said to Eran: "Don't you know what just happened?" And Eran said, "Yeah, I think he just stuck up for me." I said, "Do you realize how much courage that took?

Abal is very angry right now and could really give him a very hard time." At that instant, it really fell into place for Eran and he said: "Okay, so I guess I should say thank you. . . . Thank you." And all of us smiled. To me, that was a very meaningful event because Eran saw, on his own, that he was attacking the person, a small Arab boy, who stood up for him. This was a very important event for Eran. I'll bet you that that one encounter made quite a difference inside Eran.

Sukanya Lahiri, a facilitator, explains: "When they realize that someone [their enemy] is willing to listen to them, that is a really momentous time because people don't know what to do with their anger when somebody is listening to them." The youngsters are able to begin making a transition from demanding to be heard to hearing what the other side has to say.

"The kids go through this cycle and then are sort of like 'What now?' because they are recognizing that other people are ready to hear them. That is the time we can really reach out to them," says the facilitator.

Purged from the worries over unfairness or injustice, and enthused by the newfound relationship, the youngsters are ready to take on a new cause. When a friend reaches out across borders, that cause becomes peace.

They had just broken back into groups of eight and there was this confrontation between Sivan [an Israeli] and Bushra [a Palestinian], two good friends. . . . Another Palestinian said that all of the land, including where Israel is, is Palestine and Israelis are just occupiers of the land. Sivan's response went from what do you want to do—"Kick us out, you want us to live here? You want us to live here? You want us to leave?"—to "So what is your solution? What should the borders be? What is it? What is it?"

It was an incredibly explosive session—all of them were involved but this was between the two of them. Bushra was put on the spot—she refused to answer. And Sivan was saying, "I think there should be a Palestine, you should have your own state, you should have the West Bank, you should have Gaza, you should have most of it, but where should we be?" Bushra was silent. I said more than I usually say as a facilitator. . . . I said Sivan asked a very valid question and you need to all take the risk and tell each other what you think the solution should be. Bushra said, "Well, I am not the one who makes these decisions." I said, "This is about what you think it should be. You need to take that risk and tell each other." I said to Bushra, "You have the choice to not respond, but at some point if you want to have a real discussion, you need to say, if I were in charge, this is what I would do." In the session after . . . Bushra was able to say, "This is really, really hard for me to say but you all deserve to have the state of Israel." I am getting choked up again now because I love both of these young women. For Bushra to go from complete silence to "you deserve to have a state of Israel" is just awesome. I remember the emotion of the moment. I think Bushra was able to have a shift because I think she really loves and respects Sivan. That's awesome. That's the promise and the magic of this place.

Making Sense Out of What They Hear: Unpacking Mixed Messages

When the youngsters have begun truly to listen to one another, break-throughs come often. The youngsters begin to understand and grapple with what the other side is really thinking. One important aspect is simply clarification. They begin to decode the land mines of mixed messages that have evolved over years of conflict and mistrust. In numerous discussions throughout camp, they explore a host of symbols—symbols packed with meanings, often different, for both sides. Barbara Gottschalk tells of the different meanings such symbols can have.

> Jewelry in the form of small gold maps of Palestine [that show Israel as part of Palestine] is a permanent fixture on many, many Palestinian girls' necks. One year, we asked the Palestinian girls to explain what it means to them. To them it meant that their heart was with their homeland. It did not mean that they thought that Palestinians should take over Israel. The Israelis, however, inter-pret that piece of jewelry in the latter way; they believe that Palestinians wear the jewelry because they intend to take over Israel. For most of those girls, that isn't the meaning.

Barbara recounts another story when such symbols became a real source of conflict:

> A couple of years ago, one of the Palestinian boys came up to me. He was very frightened and said he was worried that two of the Israelis in his bunk were going to beat him up. They were angry at him and he couldn't understand why they were so angry. He had hung above his bed a flag of Palestine and the Israelis didn't want the flag there.
>
> I asked him why they didn't want the flag there but I also explained to him that things like flags and national objects were really not permitted at camp. I was wondering if he understood why they particularly didn't want it there. He said, no, he couldn't understand it all. I said, "Did you explain to them why you wanted to have the flag?" I also asked him how big it was. It was something like three by five inches. "Let's take a deep breath here and recognize that a flag is a piece of fabric. It is not like you are threatening them with a machine gun—it's a flag. But what it represents must be bothering them." And so he said, "What it represents is why I have it there." He explained his commitment

to the establishment of Palestine. I suggested to this Palestinian boy, Numan, that he should explain to the Israelis why the flag is so important to him. . . .

About an hour later some Israelis came up to me and Yaron spoke: "You know we need some help from you. We have this Palestinian boy in our bunk and he has just been hanging this great big Palestinian flag over his bed and we just won't tolerate it. It is our space too and we don't want a Palestinian flag hanging in our space where we have to look at it all the time."

So I said to them, "I think you can resolve this with the Palestinian boy. Go over to him and tell him you want to sit down and find out why it is he wants the Palestinian flag hanging over his bed. Just ask that question." So neither came back to me that day. The next day we saw the result. The crew was filming a group of Palestinians about what it was like when they first came to camp. And they were talking about what it was like—the Israelis would not let them show that they were Palestinians and that hurt them. In the film you can see, at one point the Palestinian kids decided to just jump up from their circle and go fetch one of the Israelis nearby. They picked Yaron, carried him to the circle physically, dropped him down in the middle and demanded to know is there or is there not a Palestine. He said, without hesitating, "There is no such thing as Palestine. But there should be."

It turns out they had both done exactly what I told them. They both asked each other if they could sit down and talk about why the flag was there and why some people didn't want it there. The more Numan talked about the pride in his own country and wanting to have his own country established, the more Yaron understood. He became less concerned whether it was hanging in his bunk or not and decided it was okay. They both remember this crystal clear. . . . Numan, who has returned twice as a program leader, always seems to grow a lot at Seeds of Peace.

Through unpacking the symbol and listening to one another, the youngsters achieved very real results. Yaron was ready to accept a Palestinian state. And Numan no longer feels the pressure to walk around proving his love for his country. Having been listened to, he has opened up every year and learns more and more about the other side.

Unpacking symbols takes a lot of work. Israelis worry over the meaning of the Palestinian flag, and Palestinians fear the Israeli flag. Many of our young Palestinians come to camp believing that the Star of David on the Israeli flag camouflages the Israeli dream of establishing a Jewish state stretching from the Nile River in Egypt to the Euphrates River in Iraq. Through tales passed down from their grandparents, Palestinians have learned that the blue at the top of the star means the water of the Nile and the blue at the bottom means the water of the Euphrates. Like so many stereotypes, this one contains the required iota of truth: Abraham led his flocks from Mesopotamia (Iraq) to Judea and Samaria (on the West Bank), where the Hebrews fled from Egypt and made their biblical home. But as the students speak about the symbols, both their correct interpretations and misinterpretations, they come to understand the situation far better, and they begin to make distinctions they otherwise might not be able to make.

"These two kids, they started fighting," explains a facilitator.

> They started to fight about the borders and the Palestinian said that . . . the Israeli flag—somehow they designed the borders of the greater Israel, and she was telling him that it's not true, that the flag is a very religious spot, and it has nothing to do with borders, but he's right in terms of a greater Israel. He can find it in the Torah. . . . So she agrees with him about his idea, okay, and he's just stuck with the flag, he's saying the flag is saying that, so it's amazing. . . . Her only point was, "You are right but it's not in the flag. Some of us believe in a greater Israel, but it's not on the flag." So he just insists, and when I came to him and asked him what's his point, that she agrees with him, she's saying you are right. . . . He started to listen to her, he wanted to make the point without listening to her, and I reflected that to him, that she was saying exactly what he's saying.

One-on-one discussion during coexistence session between Israeli and Palestinian Seeds

By talking about the fears that have been coiled around certain symbols or statements, by putting them on the table, the youngsters can begin to talk to one another. A counselor explained a similar process in another argument about "Palestine":

I had kids at my table argue about that . . . and the girl was saying, "I believe there should be a Palestine, I believe there will be a Palestine, but right now there's not a Palestine," and the kid, the other kid, the Palestinian kid insists, not wanting to hear, just saying that it was Palestine. And she's basically agreeing with him, and they are going in circles and in circles, saying the same thing over . . . and at some stage she said to him, "I believe there should be a Palestine, and we will give you the land," and he said, "No, you will return the land," and then she said, "Okay, we will return the land," and he said, "But . . ." and they went around again, but it was those little things where sometimes, I saw that gradually, first of all just the circling, and then all of a sudden little things that would stand out, and then back into the circling and now they're friends and I think they talk, and it's incredible to see . . . that.

Discussing symbols such as songs, flags, anthems, jewelry, and words that invoke fear or power is crucial for understanding the present meanings they convey. Consider the importance that Israel attached to the formal repudiation of several paragraphs in the thirty-year-old Palestinian Covenant—paragraphs containing words that vow to destroy the Jewish state. Even though these paragraphs had already been officially declared null and void by the Palestinian government, and Arafat himself had repeatedly said they no longer reflected the goals or the desires of his people, the Israeli government consistently demanded formal renunciation by the 535-member Palestinian National Congress (PNC). The Israeli motivation was understandable; Israelis did not know whether to believe Arafat's words or the words of the Palestinian Covenant. The Palestinian Parliament acted in 1999 to formally renounce the charter.

The Palestinian desire to explore the Torah, or the Israeli flag, is also understandable. They know that these symbols have a religious or spiritual meaning to the Israelis, and they wonder how far this should be taken. Certain members of the Israeli community may use biblical statements to support continued settlement as symbols of Hebrew identity, challenging people who disagree with them on grounds of Jewishness, not on grounds of politics. The Israeli youngsters need to talk about this with the Palestinians so that they will come to understand the distinctions the Israelis make between themselves.

One of the most recurring trigger words at camp is "Holocaust." Packed with meaning for both Israelis and Palestinians, the Holocaust is used not only to talk about the past but also to negotiate the present. Israelis are careful to use the word "Holocaust" only in reference to the systematic Nazi killings of World War II. By doing this, many youngsters are trying to make a specific point that this particular killing was unique because of why the people were killed. To an Israeli, the word "Holocaust" is a word to be applied only to the genocide the Jews experienced during World War II, when people were killed simply because of who they were. For the Jews, the word "Holocaust" represents a particular kind of evil and a particular kind of victim: the attempted extermination of an entire people, the Jewish people.

*Unpacking
Symbols*

Symbol/Trigger Word	What Israelis Hear	What Palestinians Hear
PALESTINE	The name for the entire pre-1948 British mandatory territory	The name for the Palestinian state—past, present, and future
	Does not exist	Exists under occupation
	A call for the violent destruction of Israel	The recognition of lasting peoplehood and respect

Possible Resolution: Both sides agree to use "Palestine" in the sense understood by Palestinians, but to use it alongside the phrase "coexisting with Israel"

Symbol/Trigger Word	What Israelis Hear	What Palestinians Hear
HOLOCAUST	The systematic attempt by the Nazis to exterminate the Jewish people	The excuse for *al-Nakba* (the "catastrophe" of 1948)
	A unique evil, not comparable to *al-Nakba*	A term applicable to the suffering experienced by Palestinians

Possible Resolution: Both sides agree to use "Holocaust" in the sense understood by Israelis, but to use it alongside the phrase "does not justify *al-Nakba*"

Many Palestinians, however, make an explicit point of using the word "Holocaust" to apply to their own situation as victims of oppression. They feel they must do this because their suffering must be given appropriate weight or else they will have sacrificed their claim to equal rights. Since the Holocaust is often cited as the reason why so many Jews came to the area and as the chief causal factor for the creation of the State of Israel, it is therefore understood as a large reason for *al-Nakba*, the "catastrophe" of

1948. If the Palestinians use a different word, or allow the Jews to claim sole right to the word, it is tantamount to allowing the Jews to claim sole right to victimhood. The Palestinians feel they must use the word or else it appears linguistically justifiable to say that the Holocaust was a valid reason for their displacement; after all, a Palestinian believes a Jew will say, "There was only one Holocaust."

We can see just such an argument between Yoyo and Laith, an Israeli and a Palestinian, and their facilitator:

Laith:	For me as a person I don't care how many people died. I believe if someone, if people have suffered that's enough. For me the death of one person is a Holocaust.
Yoyo:	You say if a person dies, it doesn't matter if he dies because of war or something like that? Clarify your point.
Laith:	I'm telling you that for me the number is not important. The only difference between the six million . . . I'm telling you that the number is not the important thing. What is important is not the number of people killed. . . .
Facilitator:	Try to put yourself in their shoes. Why do you think it would matter to the Jews? You say for you the number doesn't matter. You know it is a sensitive topic and it matters for the Jews. So why do you think it matters?
Laith:	I'm saying in general. I'm trying to pretend I'm a Jew, putting myself in their shoes. Why does the number matter? Why? I want to hear from Yoyo. Why?
Yoyo:	Forget the number. Just think about the concept of taking a whole people—putting them on trains, sending them to a place somewhere in Poland or, for that matter, anywhere, putting them into gas chambers because you hate those people, because you can't bear the thought that they exist. With all due respect, this is not the thing that happens to the Palestinians.

The exchange between Laith and Yoyo was particularly significant because they already shared a relationship with each other. There was a basis for trust. When Laith struggled to understand why the number mattered so much, he said, "I want to hear from Yoyo." He trusted he would receive an answer he could believe—even if it was not one he could agree with. When Laith said, "I'm telling you that for me the number is not important. The only difference between the six million . . ." and broke off in mid-sentence, he was acknowledging the number "six million" perhaps for the first time in his life. Other Palestinians claim they are taught that only twenty thousand Jews were killed or that the Holocaust never happened or, if it did, it was the fault of the Jews. In one coexistence session in 1999, a Palestinian said he had learned that the Holocaust was "when the rich Jews killed the poor Jews so they could go to Israel."

Laith and Yoyo

Laith and Yoyo were two youngsters from the original camp in 1993. Both big kids and stuck in the same facilitation session, they took to arguing with each other right away. Laith had arrived consumed with anger, demanding that the Jews go back from where they came—to Europe. It was only after camp, recalled Yoyo, that Laith agreed that "we, the twenty Israelis who had taken part in camp, could remain in the country—under a Palestinian government." The story of their relationship parallels the journey of each of our youngsters.

The turning point in Laith's development occurred during his first summer. The Holocaust was raised during an early coexistence session. Laith said that he was taught that only twenty thousand Jews had been killed. "I did not know it was a genocide." He told the Israelis in the workshop that even if it was a genocide, "it does not justify taking my land, taking my home, taking my shelter, and throwing me in a refugee camp." Elad, an Israeli, started to sob when he spoke of his grandparents who had perished in the Holocaust. "You weren't even born when they died," retorted Laith. "How can you cry for someone you didn't even know? You should cry for me. I am the one who is suffering right now, not your grandfather. I am the one who sees people getting shot. I am the one who sees refugee camps." When the argument turned to the number of victims, Laith declared, "I don't think six million were killed." The workshop broke up in hysterics. Tears cascaded down the cheeks of Israelis while prideful Palestinians sat in disgust. Both delegations stormed out.

Later that day David Allyn, a facilitator, brought Laith a copy of *Night*, Elie Wiesel's account of his life in a concentration camp. "David started talking to me," Laith recalled. "The first thing he said was just listen, you don't have to be convinced, just try to understand the other side's point of view." During rest hour, Laith read a few pages of *Night*. He started to cry. When Elad emerged from the infirmary the next day (he had developed a fever), Laith spotted him. He walked up to Elad, raised up his right hand, and gave him a high five. Only much later did we discover that Elad Wiesel was a cousin of Elie Wiesel.

A week later the Israeli delegation left for home. The Palestinians and other Arab delegations had seen them off at the Washington, D.C., National Airport and were traveling back into the District of Columbia. The chartered bus crossed the 14th Street Bridge and was passing the Holocaust Museum. Barbara Gottschalk pointed it out to Laith, who said he would like to tour the museum. It surprised everyone. "All the guys wanted to go shopping but I had heard about the Holocaust Museum," he said. "It's like the best Holocaust museum in the world. You can get lots of information there." So, accompanied by two other Arab teenagers, Laith took a guided tour. Reflecting on his experience, Laith said later: "I think everyone must go to the Holocaust Museum. I mean I think I learned something. I enjoyed it. It's not like going to a movie but I liked going there to get information. We should learn that what happened should not happen again to any people. Even to the Israelis. If we [the Palestinians] have the power now to do things like that, I would never do it. I would just go and shake hands with them."

After that, Laith and Yoyo became fast friends, and every delegation of Arabs and Israelis now visits the museum before returning home. Laith's step led Yoyo to take similar risks in their relationship. He often invited Laith to go horseback riding with him and to have dinner at his Jerusalem home even though he knew his father, a wounded Israeli war hero, would retreat to the basement whenever the Palestinian came to visit. After Jericho was "liberated" from Israeli rule, Laith invited his Israeli friend to tour the West Bank town. It was illegal for Israelis to go to Jericho without special permission. But Laith's father promised him they would be safe. As they went through the checkpoint, leaving Israeli-controlled territory, the car was stopped. "Don't worry," Laith's father told the soldiers. "I'm just showing Jericho to my two sons." Following his return home, says Yoyo, Laith amended his earlier proviso that only the Israeli campers who had been at Seeds of Peace could remain in Palestine. He agreed that "our families could also remain here." Now, says Yoyo, "he believes in a solution comprising two states—Israeli and Palestinian."

Their story is the story of change at Seeds of Peace. The youngsters come into coexistence discussions fearful and ready to fight. As they share their thoughts they learn to uncover their own hatred; they are prideful in their attacks on one another, unending in their rebuttals. The youngsters offer a barrage of defenses—they debate anything to keep from simply accepting "the other's" views. As they push one another to an emotional clash, facilitators help ensure that they turn to the pain that they are trying to share but find difficult to discuss in such open surroundings. Finding a way to share this suffering with one another, they are able to see and feel firsthand that their own pain is much like that of their enemies. Given an opportunity to be accepted by the enemy, by as simple a gesture as a high five, the youngsters open up to each other, no longer pressured to prove their own righteousness. As they listen to one another's stories, argue over actions, and decode the symbols of the enemy, they learn that peace is possible and that solutions can indeed be found. When they are listened to, they listen. When they listen to one another, they are already working together. In the words of one facilitator:

> I saw the kids fighting . . . fighting I mean in the sessions, in the appropriate way. Each one of them stands on his point of view, is not willing to listen to the other side, even to be quiet, but I've had the feeling that he doesn't really think about the other side and about the needs of the other side. He just sticks with his own, with his own needs, with his own pain, or whatever. And then to see this, these guys making some switching, and all of a sudden they open, and to see them somehow through the process sitting together, trying to find solutions and they did!

> I know, they're not going to solve the Middle East problem right now, but to see how these kids move from one point of resistance and I can sometimes say of hatred, okay, moving to the other point where they really opened themselves to each other and trying to find a way, where both parties can be happy with some solution, it's amazing. It's amazing.

The Crisis

The Process of Healing

All the pressures and opportunities at camp that allow for such progress do not, however, always work together so smoothly. Often the love, support, and opportunity for personal expression can become walls to hide behind while the youngsters bottle up many of their true feelings. Noticing when the students are doing this, either consciously or subconsciously, is always a difficult job, but as the weeks begin to fall away and we have come to know the campers better, it sometimes becomes clear that many of them are not owning up to their real feelings. The tonic for this, in years past, has been the entrance of some sort of crisis, a time when some event forces the youngsters to be up front with their emotions. If we take poker as an analogy for discussing conflict, then the crisis forces them to show their hands. It reminds them that their work cannot be done if they hide from one another, and it gives them a new opportunity to reach out to one another when they least expect it.

Partly because of the intensity of a crisis situation, the youngsters often need encouragement here as well—to remind them that the best of the options is not to dismiss the possibilities of making peace, but to take on the challenge more bluntly. If they fail to pull together now, in this moment of crisis, and find whatever binds them as human beings, the whole process will fail, and all that they have invested in building trust and friendship will dissipate. It is this sudden sense of both disillusion and danger that compels them to make the massive effort to discover their humanity. "As human beings," says facilitator Sukanya Lahiri, "we connect with a sense of other people's pain. If you see someone being shot on TV, I think most people's initial instinct is 'Oh my gosh!' The crisis takes us to another level of 'Oh my gosh!' to 'That could have been so and so!' or 'Oh my gosh, he was just like my brother!'"

Two types of crises have emerged—one is an internal crisis, the other external. An internal crisis results from a situation that develops at the camp because of circumstances that arise within the nascent community. The latter is caused by "real-world" pressures, which cannot be ignored at camp—for example, a terrorist bombing back home. In both cases, the crisis causes each side to fall back from its new positions of trust, understanding, and friendship to its pre-camp positions of mistrust, stereotypes, and fear. However, this position is not exactly as it was before their camp experiences; now they have an intimate knowledge of one another, as well as insight into their way of thinking and understanding of the conflict. This newfound knowledge and compassion often means these old attitudes do not sit well with the campers. They feel betrayed by responses of their counterparts. Having seen what can be accomplished, the campers now feel that their relationships are in jeopardy; to be friends again will take a concerted effort of honesty and expression. This process not only reinvigorates the relationship but develops it further, to the point that it becomes valuable to each side—something that they are willing to defend.

Confronting Fear and Horror

In 1997, the crisis occurred on July 30, the eleventh day of camp. "We were having breakfast. Suddenly some Israeli girls were crying. We didn't know what happened," recalled Hiba, a Palestinian. During breakfast on this chilly Wednesday morning, Israeli parents were calling their children with reports of a terrorist attack, a bombing in the central vegetable market, the Mahane Yehuda, in downtown Jerusalem. Rumors spread quickly, creating a sense of near panic among the sixty Israelis. All of them wanted to use the phones to find out if members of their family had been hurt or just to hear a comforting voice. We did not permit that. Instead, I called Frank Sesno, a former colleague at CNN, to find out exactly what had happened and asked the entire camp to assemble in the Big Hall. By the time I got there, the Israelis were all on one side of the gym facing the stage and the Palestinians were on the other. The Israelis, looking confused and scared, had huddled together in small groups. They had their arms around each other and were sobbing loudly. "I felt that the Israelis now, okay, they will start hating us," said Hiba. "When they are in a safe haven and then they are thrown back into the real world," explained Sukanya, "a lot of kids are going to try to shut down this experience because it is too painful and it is dangerous."

The outside world had come crashing in on us with all its fury. I wanted all the campers to feel the full brunt of the horror. "You never know how tough it is to make peace until something very terrible happens. Something terrible has happened," I announced. "It is going to test every single one of us. You are going to have to show some real understanding and compassion. Who knows what the word 'compassion' means?" An Israeli raised her hand. "Compassion is when you feel someone else's sadness," she said. Again, I tried to turn this very ugly incident into something that could motivate both sides to become more honest with each other. "This is going to be a test of every single one of you," I repeated. "It will test whether the sound of peace can be louder than the horror of war." Then I told them what had happened. Two suicide bombers dressed as religious Jews had blown themselves up in the marketplace, taking the lives of thirteen innocent civilians and injuring forty more (later it was learned that 170 had been hurt). The terrorists were members of the Palestinian group Hamas. There was an audible gasp. "This is not the first time it's happened. It's not the first time that Israelis have been killed," I said. Even though there were no civilian Palestinian casualties, I wanted to be fair. Palestinians often complain at camp that when they are killed, their deaths are ignored by the media. So I added, "It's not the first time Palestinians have been killed. As you know, Arabs were killed in their mosque in Hebron. There have been Arabs who have been killed by Israelis." No one, I told them, should be afraid of venting their feelings. That was what Seeds of Peace was all about, creating a place where everyone would feel safe displaying their feelings to the other side. "When things like this happen, it is very natural to feel two emotions: anger at the other side and fear," I said. Then I set the challenge for each of them: "Obviously this is not going to have a positive impact on the peace talks. But our little group here now becomes the only place where a message of hope can be sent to the world. This afternoon there will be a reporter from the Associated Press here and there will be a camera crew," I announced. I told them that if they did not want to speak with them, they should not. The reporters would respect their privacy. "The only reason we are letting them come is so that our work is not forgotten." The media presence also helped to underscore what was at stake and the importance of the challenge they faced.

Then I began to engage them in a dialogue at first with me and then with one another. What can we learn from this? I asked. George, a Palestinian, raised his hand. "The only way we can stop these bombings is that we make peace," he said. How can we continue in the face of such attacks? "We should be stronger than they are. We should say 'yes' to peace and 'no' to these bombings. We should try harder to make peace. That's the only way," George said. Gilly, an Israeli, stood up. "I believe I'm speaking for all of us when I say none of us holds a grudge against any one of you." That was the icebreaker. The Palestinians now visibly sighed in relief. "All of us want peace," added Gilly. "We have nothing against you." A few campers applauded. Then Sari, a Palestinian, raised her hand. "We are sorry for what happened and we are sharing your grief," she said. An Egyptian added, "You are now experiencing the pain. We should not forget it but help each other to work through it." Ihab, a Palestinian, wanted the floor. "Hurry up and make peace. Not to wait more and more," he said. Then Ruba stood. "I want to send my condolences. I hope that if we work together such acts will stop." Amgad, an Egyptian, added, "The Israelis who are here do not have guns. They are not soldiers. The Palestinians who are here are not terrorists. Not in this place. That's what we need to realize." Then another Palestinian stood. "I am crying," he said, "because we are human beings and the people who killed are human beings. I'm very sorry . . ." and his voice trailed off.

For the first time I noticed that several Palestinians were crying. "I was sitting with my Israeli friend, and I don't know why, I started to cry, just . . . I don't know why," said Hiba. "Then I said to myself, okay, many Palestinian people were killed too, so I didn't care. But at that moment I cared, and I cried really from my heart, because I said, okay they are human beings like us, and look at my friends, they are crying. It wasn't easy to do that. But what happened, all of them, they were sharing sadness, the Arabs and the Israelis, so at that moment I felt the meaning of friendship, of real friendship."

It was time to let them go and do the important work they had to do, first consoling each other and then rebuilding the relationships. We asked everyone to report to his or her coexistence group on the big lawn outside. The facilitators would dismiss the Israelis from each group in an orderly manner that would allow all of them to call home. Campers with families in Jerusalem would be excused first. As the afternoon passed, an eerie calm returned; some youngsters sang quietly with James Durst, our resident folksinger, while others played baseball or just talked. But one

Israeli girl continued to cry hysterically. She said she had not even tried to call home because she knew her mother would not be home. She had gone to Jerusalem for a job interview that day in a building near the marketplace. Fortunately, neither she nor anyone else's family was injured in the attack. But the impact was almost as devastating as if she had been there.

Hazem, a Palestinian, said that several Israelis told him they wanted to go home. He understood their desire. "I said no, you have to stay because the Palestinians must understand your pain. You need to stay and face the facts," he said. "You have to realize that you are not the only person in the world. The Israelis don't live by themselves. They are in the Middle East. Every human being suffers, especially the Palestinians." He explained that Seeds of Peace "seemed like a dream, a fantasy, a bubble where Israelis and Palestinians can live and coexist together. When the bombing occurred, the bubble blew up. The dream fell apart. Like when you have a good dream and you wake up and reality begins again. I told them that the way to face difficulties is to face it, stick where you are. In those moments you need to show that you feel you are Israeli. I said you need to feel like patriots, even more than you used to be."

Many Israelis didn't want to go to the coexistence sessions. They didn't want to share their pain with the other side. It was, perhaps, too threatening. "They made us try to go to facilitation groups and I just didn't want to. After John's speech, none of the Israelis were there. We needed to be together," Gilly explained. But we insisted that they spend this time with the Palestinians. If the Israelis went to comfort each other and forgot about the Palestinians, they would miss the chance of seeing Palestinians share their pain. When they did go to coexistence groups together, each side was able to connect and grow. Palestinians found themselves connecting with the Israelis' pain; Israelis found that they could truly open up to the enemy. "They got to see that we suffer too, the big Israelis, the occupiers, etcetera etcetera, we suffer too. . . . They got to see Israelis crying, not only Palestinian suffering and crying. We're people, we're human beings, too, you know. We have families. Maybe now they can think about the bombings as maybe one of my Israeli friends died there, you know . . . I think it was good for camp. I don't think anything was worse. The coexistence was quieter, calm. It was a tiring day," said Shira.

By the next morning, the Palestinians had posted a handwritten placard at the entrance to the Big Hall. It read:

Dear Friends,

We the Palestinian delegation share your sorrow and oppose terror against innocent civilians from both sides. We must work together to stand against those who are against peace from both sides and support every effort that leads us to achieve peace. Once again, nothing can stop us from making peace, so we must all pray for those who were killed or injured and pray also for peace.

The Palestinian Delegation

The best response to the crisis wasn't always clear. There was a debate about whether the Seeds of Peace flag should be lowered to half-mast. The Palestinians opposed this, explaining that their suffering was constant and daily, and such a move would insult the ongoing Palestinian suffering. But on a personal level, there was no question that the events of July 30 galvanized both sides to feel for each other. Through the Israeli group mourning, each side was able to use the bombing to establish its legitimacy as victims in the eyes of the other side, propelling the process forward. They had won something when they won the other's sympathy. They also came face to face with their own guilt about being at a peace camp during such a horrible attack on their people. Many expressed this guilt at the time, and then the youngsters were able to talk about it and work through it. Israelis had also discovered something important—that Palestinians could grieve for them. That touched them and rendered the process human. More important, it allowed the Israelis thereafter to open up and feel for the plight of the Palestinians.

Confronting Rage and Anger

The crisis that occurred in 1998 precipitated a similar breakthrough, but it was more difficult to work through. The delegations arrived thoroughly briefed by their governments and consequently more intent on provoking each other. The weight of what Professor Stanley Walzer calls the "contextual realities"—the situation that affects the psychological baggage brought by the campers—was greater than ever. The Israeli-Palestinian peace process had virtually collapsed; Arab countries had reduced their ties with Israel to protest Prime Minister Netanyahu's hard-line policies; the United Nations had voted to seat "Palestine" in the General Assembly; and the attention of the United States, the only country capable of brokering a deal, seemed diverted by the scandal involving President Clinton and Monica Lewinsky. "The big difference is the amount of anger and hate," noted Walzer. "They are more keen and eager to defend their parochial national interests and less willing to give those up to reach a new common ground. The pressures and attitudes are more severe but the contextual pressure is quite severe, so you arrive at camp with a functional capacity that is quite diminished."

The governments also seemed worried about the impact that Seeds of Peace could have on their participants. The Israeli foreign ministry, for example, took the Israeli participants on a five-day retreat to teach them the "facts" about who was to blame for the failure of the Oslo peace process. They were reminded that they were chosen as official envoys and that they should be careful not to embarrass their government. Several of the teenagers told us that tight alliances were formed during the retreat, affecting the development of interdelegation alliances when they arrived at camp. The Palestinians had also held a retreat. Their youngsters were given similar instructions and brought to meet President Yasser Arafat before their departure. In short, when they arrived both sides were pre-pared to trade insults and continue fighting the battles being waged by their leaders at home.

The crisis was provoked by the visit of a high-ranking Israeli parliamen-tarian. Meir Sheetrit, the leader of the governing Likud coalition in the Israeli Knesset, wanted to see the camp in operation. Seeds of Peace has welcomed visits from ambassadors of many nations and did so proudly with this important guest. What was not anticipated was the damage that he could inflict almost overnight. Sheetrit was asked by one of the more hawk-ish Israeli escorts to meet with his delegation. The youngsters wanted to know whether they could discuss Jerusalem with their Palestinian counter-parts. He told them Jerusalem is not negotiable and never will be. It is the undivided capital of the Jewish state and will always remain so.

In their coexistence workshops the next day, the Israelis took a new hard line. When the Palestinians reminded them that their former leader, the late Yitzhak Rabin, had already agreed to negotiate over Jerusalem and signed a pact at Oslo incorporating that pledge, many of the Israelis became even more upset. Less than twenty-four hours later, the Palestinians found a way to retaliate. It came during "Culture Night," when each of the dele-gations performs traditional dances and music from their nations for the entire camp. In previous summers, songs about Jerusalem had proved so contentious that I had asked the Israelis and Palestinians to forgo includ-ing them or any other "political" material. I was pleased when the Israeli escorts told me that there was nothing political in their repertoire and no mention of Jerusalem. But I learned that the Palestinians were preparing to sing a song about Jerusalem. When I asked their escort to forgo the song, pointing out that the Israelis had already agreed to abide by the rules, he said that was impossible. His delegation had prepared only two numbers, a folk dance and the song, and it was too late to dissuade them. Not to worry, he assured me, the song was purely religious in nature and wouldn't offend anyone.

One by one, the delegations performed their beautifully costumed and exuberant dances, with a drumbeat punctuating their rhythmic clapping and pounding of feet. The Egyptians began with a sensuous belly dance greeted by wild applause and raucous dancing on the gym floor. Now, it was the Israeli delegation's turn. They began with the hora, the famous circle dance, catapulting campers high into the air on a chair and thrusting them up and down. The Israeli Arabs then performed their version of the dabka, a traditional foot-stomping Arab dance, while legions of youngsters snaked their way along the floor. The next song, they announced, would honor the memory of a girl killed "in an attack at [Tel Aviv's] Dizengoff Center" on March 4, 1996, "the date of her fifteenth birthday." Her diary had been discovered following her death, and in it the words for a song. The girls were dressed in simple white dresses, the boys in white T-shirts and jeans. All of them had small blue-and-white handkerchiefs tied like sashes around their wrists and one boy waved a homemade Israeli flag drawn on a plain piece of paper. Accompanied by a single guitar, they spoke young Bat-Chen Shahak's words, "A Poem of Peace."

> I would like to talk about peace.
> Every person has a dream
> One wants to be a millionaire
> Another wants to be a writer
> And I have a dream about peace.
>
> Maybe I'm just an innocent girl.
> But is it too much to ask for peace and security?
> Is it too much to dream of walking securely in the streets of the Old City?
> Is it too much to dream of not seeing mothers of young soldiers crying
>   over their graves?

There was polite applause. Then came the announcement that Bat-Chen's mother had created a scholarship in her daughter's memory for an Israeli to annually attend the Seeds of Peace program. I felt conflicted. Part of me wanted to rush the stage and yell foul. It was clear that the murdered Israeli had died as a result of a terrorist attack even though the Israelis had not used the word "terrorist." The poem also described her dream of walking securely in the Old City, a reference to Jerusalem, and concluded with the allusion of tears for the martyrs killed in the ongoing war to defend Israel. The song violated the prohibition against introducing politics into the cultural evening. But how could I interrupt such a solemn occasion, particularly after Bat-Chen's mother had agreed to provide a scholarship? The Israelis would never understand that their moving tribute to her memory constituted "politics." I chose to remain silent. But a storm was brewing.

The eruption came a few minutes later when, after the Moroccans, the Palestinians took the stage. After a boisterous dance, they performed the song about Jerusalem. As they began, the Israeli delegation leaders rushed to my side ready to pounce on any phrase, any word that broke the informal accord. I asked one of the Arab Israeli escorts to translate for me. The song skirted the boundary between religion and politics. Its first verses spoke of "the city of prayer, the most beautiful rose of all cities . . . our eyes travel between the holy places and hug the old churches and mosques." It spoke of "God's merciful face," but as it continued it became more and more clear that the song was a lament to a lost city, a paean to the brave Arab soldiers who fought and lost control of Arab East Jerusalem in the June 1967 war.

> The child is in the cave with his mother Mary.
> Their two faces are crying for the homeless people, for the children
> Without homes and for those who died in defending the city of peace.
> When Jerusalem fell, our love went away.

And as the song continued, it became clear that it was not just a lament but a promise to avenge the loss. As they sang, one Palestinian (who later said he had rushed to his bunk after he saw the homemade Israeli flag) waved the Palestinian flag.

> The strong rage is coming.
> The strong rage is coming.
> The strong rage is coming and I am full of faith.
> The strong rage is coming and it will overcome my sadness.
> From every direction it is coming and will beat the powerful side.
> My country's gates will not close for I am coming to pray.
> I will knock on the gates and they will open for me.
> The Jordan River will wash my face.
> And you, the Jordan, will rinse away the barbarian's tracks.

After they finished, there was wild applause from the predominantly Arab audience as shouts of "Palestine" went forth from the stage. The word "barbarian" caught in the Israeli craw. There was no mistaking who was meant. But the entire song, sung by Palestinians wrapped in black-and-white kaffiyehs waving in the air, had the power of a battle cry. I later learned that the song was written by the popular Lebanese singer Fairouz. It was a huge hit in 1970 because it bemoaned the loss of Jerusalem in the 1967 war. It has since become a virtual anthem for the Palestinians and is known by both Israelis and Arabs as a song that captures the emotion of the conflict for the Palestinians. The Israelis were furious. Some of them were crying. Others simply felt betrayed by those they thought were friends. I feared that war might break out at camp but also knew that if I did nothing, it definitely would.

Mounting the stage, I spoke candidly of my despair and disappointment in everyone. I was angry and it showed. It was demonstrations like the ones we had seen on stage, I told them, that would ensure more warfare. The corpses, however, would be theirs. "Just look around you," I said. "If you cannot find a way to stop this madness, half of you may never return to Seeds of Peace." I spoke of my own health problems, how I had recently had a cancer scare and (getting on my knees) I told them how grateful I was to be alive. "You have one chance in life and this is it." What would happen in the remaining week of camp was up to them. But let there be no illusions about the job they had at hand—or what I expected of them. As they left to return to their bunks, there was muted conversation but mostly silence. I hoped my blunt words had brought them to the edge of the precipice. I hoped they would look down and see the abyss that awaited them.

The shock treatment worked but it took time. The delegation leaders, who at first refused to talk to one another, eventually drafted a joint statement that they read at lineup the next afternoon. It called on their successors to share the programs they intend to present on Culture Night. "If we review each other's programs we will better anticipate each other's sensitivities and avoid some of the discomfort, pain, and misunderstanding of last night's program. This will give the leaders the opportunity to reconsider selections should they cause offense to others," the statement said. It concluded: "We urge the campers to proceed in their efforts towards coexistence during the days we have left. We came here to find a way to speak to one another and coexist with one another. We do not want to be distracted from this important mission."

Nonetheless, it took several days to recover. The Palestinians protested that the Israelis had started the conflict by their overtly political song and waving their flag. Furthermore, the Palestinians were angry because they no longer perceived me as neutral and fair-minded. At lineup the next day, I publicly apologized for putting them so squarely in the dock, for blaming them for the breakdown. For the next few hours, however, they continued to insist that their song was religious and not political. But they knew they were part of the provocateurs. Everyone now was forced to deal with the crisis and the real-world hatred it had aroused. In the coexistence workshops, they spoke to one another more candidly than ever. And they listened not only newly intent on what each side was saying but with a heightened desire to find a solution. For the next three days, arguments broke out all over camp, in the dining hall, on the sides of soccer fields; it seemed that there was always an argument somewhere. But in arguing it out, they learned to deal with it and went through the facilitation process again—this time even facilitating themselves.

What provoked this new round of heavy discussions seemed to be the realization that they had not been completely honest and forthright until the crisis. The crisis allows for some more hidden feelings to be publicly displayed. In 1997, the crisis expressed the very deep feeling among Israelis that they—not the Palestinians—are the real victims. The bombing allowed them, and indeed almost forced them, to reveal this sentiment starkly. They publicly showed some of their most important and treasured feelings at the time; they showed their zeitgeist. And when they talked about their guilt of being at camp, they finally talked about some of their most reserved feelings, allowing Palestinians to hear the full force of their emotions, and allowing Israelis to work through those emotions. In a crisis, the campers come face to face with some of their own more personal feelings and at the same time come face to face with the fact that they have not been perfectly expressing them. In 1998, they again found themselves in a situation where they were expressing feelings they had been suppressing. This time the feelings were a little more confrontational. That may have been a result of the changed attitude in the region, or their heightened preparedness and readiness to do battle (the contextual realities), or simply may have been a different facet of the same bundle of feelings that are within the hearts of each of our campers almost every year.

Certainly, no feelings they have are isolated single feelings—that is, during a crisis we do not try to tap into "the secret feeling" that is in the heart of each child. We do hope, however, to get them to come face to face with some aspect of those feelings and come to the realization that they may not yet have given it adequate voice. This may also explain why many of the youths feel so hopeless during times of crises. They may be thinking that there is no ample space to share those feelings—though of course there is and it is the job of the facilitators, counselors, and staff to ensure that they find this space very soon afterward. The crisis, then, breaks down into four basic parts: *crisis*—an event forces the campers to express feelings together that are very close to their hearts; *acknowledgment*—someone shows the campers that this is not what have been doing up until then; *inspiration*—someone steers them toward the work in front of them and does not allow them to become fatalistic about camp or the process, or to fall back to their pre-camp positions; and *exploration*—the youngsters share and build upon their new honesty with one another.

The fact that the crisis is a group phenomenon is perhaps most important. Expressing deep feelings alone in a coexistence workshop can seem fleeting or unsatisfactory—especially because the content of many of the feelings revolves around a group idea: "we are suffering," "we love (and stand together in our love of) Jerusalem," and so forth. When all the youngsters are upset, it becomes easier to express those feelings that, they worry, might make them seem "anti-peace." Many of the students are also afraid of breaking delicate friendships, so they refrain from asking their toughest or most heartfelt questions. The crisis brings all of this into the open. The group pressure is to share, and then to argue. This group effort allows the youngsters even more room to explore.

Why not, if the crisis is so productive, be in a state of constant crisis? Peacemaking is an active process and one that involves more than simply sharing these deep feelings. Normal relations are needed for most of the work to be accomplished both before and after the crisis. And obviously, though it may be productive, a crisis is not always a positive experience for the youngsters. Many fear for their families in times of violence, or feel let down by their friends in times of arrogance. In essence, the crisis is no different from the rest of camp; the only difference is that it is a compressed response to a heightened incident. We have little choice in how to deal with it: The social norms and philosophy of Seeds of Peace dictate that we let the youngsters fully express themselves. Our job in guiding them is to make sure that this expression is properly dealt with—that there is ample time for them to express the emotions that surface during the crisis and to share those emotions with one another. We try to make sure they remain dedicated to understanding and caring for one another, and make sure we allow them the space to do that. When we do, many of the campers feel that it is a defining moment in their experience at camp—when they feel the full brunt of their own negative feelings and yet are still able to overcome them.

Striking a chord—
Palestinian Seed
with Israeli
bunkmates

The Color Games

Building a Team

There is another, far different, kind of crisis that we make sure to create every year—the Color Games. Set near the last days of camp, we whip all the campers into a frenzy of excitement and then split them down the line into two huge teams. For two and a half days the youngsters compete against each other in an enormous variety of ways—from soccer and sailing to singing and artwork. They wake early in the morning for group tug-of-war and canoe races. They sit on different sides of the dining hall during meals. They drop the (by then) well-worn green Seeds of Peace shirts and don the colors of their new team, augmenting their "uniform" with face paint, ribbons, and hairspray. Each team is given six counselors to organize them and to stress the importance of the event, the teamwork needed, the honor won in victory, and the integrity kept in defeat.

The games, though ostensibly focused around competition, are the final push by the staff to stress the closeness that each camper can feel toward any other. And they are one last chance to fuel the youngsters' sense of confidence before they go home. Anybody can achieve great things in the Color Games. Each camper is given a spot on an "All Star" team and slotted to compete in their very best activities. As they compete in event after event, their teammates drop by to cheer them on, most shouting so much that by the second day they have lost their voices. The cheering and companionship end up being some of the greatest moments for the campers. It cuts to the heart of caring for someone regardless of their identity—to think of someone as an Israeli or a Palestinian during the games is almost unthinkable. Each team becomes a family, with the youngsters running to get water for each other, celebrating victories together, and walking hand in hand after a close loss to the other team. For many, it is the best experience of camp.

"What happened was that I was on the green team and we had 'Message to Garcia' [the final event that involves every member of both teams]," recalled Hiba, a Palestinian. "I was the last player and my number was 84. I had to memorize the poem. Sultan was

Color Games tug of war competition

from Jordan and he had to do the same thing for the blue team. It was the hardest moment of my life, to memorize it because it was long. My team said to me, don't worry, it's only words. But I had to say it in front of the whole camp, and in front of Tim [camp director Tim Wilson], and when I did it, and we won, everyone started to cry. I couldn't believe myself. I couldn't speak even. I wanted to cry too. So it was the best moment. Not at the camp—of my life."

For other Palestinians, such as Bushra, the Color Games made palpable a coexistence she thought could exist only in her dreams. It validated her as a person who was fully equal to the Israelis. "I felt great because I was playing on the same team. It is such a great feeling to be on the same team with Israelis, and the other team is Palestinians and Israelis." One of the green team coaches recalled that he asked a Palestinian in the relay races to step aside so that an Israeli, who was a stronger swimmer, could take his place. The coach realized only later what he was asking the Palestinian to do. As the Israeli dove into the water, his team, the green, was lagging behind. Being the stronger swimmer, however, the Israeli managed to catch up and win. In that moment, the Palestinian turned to his coach and said he felt as if he had won the race. The coach told him he had.

When the games come to a close, the two teams gather on the lakeside beach. As the scores are read off, the winning team is announced, and amid raucous cheering and hugging, the winning team jumps in the lake first. Slowly the other team is allowed in, and as they all come together in the water, the Color Games are forgotten, but the friendships are not. Noa, an Israeli, wrote this song about the end:

> When I look into your eyes, I feel like part of the green team
> But then I ask myself, what does that really mean?
> Because a few days ago you were a Seed of Peace like me
> But now things have changed, can't you see?
>
> We belong to different sides. I am green and you are blue
> And during Color Games, I behaved as if I didn't know you
> Because a few days ago, you were a Seed of Peace like me
> But now things have changed, can't you see?
>
> Now the game is coming to an end and the whole thing is through
> I know I want you back as a friend even though you were blue
> Because a few days ago you were a Seed of Peace like me
> But now things have changed, can't you see?

The youngsters accept each other as friends again, though this time with bragging rights. "My team lost, and for the first time in many years I felt tears in my eyes," recalled Hazem, a Jordanian teenager. "The person I took comfort in was an Israeli who had been my partner in a canoe race that morning. When both teams were in the lake, all was forgotten and the entire camp was united, hugging and congratulating each other on the best two and a half days of their lives."

In the 1999 Color Games, the blue team wrote a song that they performed during the talent competition. It epitomizes what they learned during their three weeks together:

> We come to camp all different nations,
> Mistrust and fear have explanations;
> After years, a lifetime of fight,
> Came in thinking "We must prove we're right."
>
> After a while we take more chances,
> Look within and challenge our stances,
> Begin to see what was always in place,
> That the enemy, too, has a face.
>
> *Chorus:*
> Now we are here, Color Games busy,
> Blue versus green, winning ain't easy;
> When we go home, this flame will still burn:
> Our leaders will have much to learn!
>
> We can create one nation overcoming the past,
> With a vision of hope that is much brighter,
> Building friendships and memories that will forever last;
> We can rise to the top where we'll shout:
> "Stand together!"

Returning Home

Fighting for Peace

When the Color Games are finished and the bags are packed, saying good-bye is as difficult as it is necessary, and the youngsters leave in tear-filled buses as they file out to the airport. "When we were saying good-bye, we couldn't imagine that we were going to leave each other and never see each other. It's just something that you don't know. . . . It's something in here that you feel; it's hurting you," said Ibrahim, a Palestinian. He said it was a very sad moment but also one of the best "because at that moment we knew that we became a family."

But as camp comes to an end for them, the experience does not. Now they face the difficult task of coming home to their old families and friends. To be sure, they've made new friends, but has this been an experience that changes the way they see the Middle East? Are they truly any different than when they left?

Ultimately, the impact of Seeds of Peace on the region hangs on this question. For when they go home, the youngsters are once again faced with the old environments of hate and prejudice. Should they keep their opinions, many will be hurt by the negative reactions encountered from people they assumed would support them. Experiences of rejection, isolation, blame, and ridicule are common, explains Barbara Gottschalk, who says these youngsters join the ranks of "traitors" throughout history who have dared to look at their enemies as fellow human beings.

Coming Home to Rejection and Ridicule

When they return home, the youngsters must ask themselves a very difficult question: Should they shut down the experiences they've had at Seeds of Peace and fold back into their old communities, or should they acknowledge their new opinions and fight to change the communities around them? Their answer, for the most part, has been astounding.

"When I went home, I was very happy because I was going to tell the people what happened to me. And first I expected that they would be happy too. But everything was completely different," says Hiba, a Palestinian camper from 1997. Her friends said she had been brainwashed. At school she was suddenly regarded as an outsider. "Hiba, what's wrong with you?" asked her classmates when she talked about her experience at Seeds of Peace. Amgad found the reintegration into Egyptian society and into family life very difficult. "The hardest part for me is when I sit at home and watch the news and it says the Israeli soldiers did this, or the Israeli government did that, and when I read the newspapers and they condemn everything Israeli," he explained. "Every day I'm bombarded, pressured into hating these people by others. I've been called a 'traitor' by many people, by my friends and some people I meet in the street." Even Amgad's brother and uncle were upset when letters postmarked in Israel started arriving at their home. "My brother works for the government, and so whenever I get letters from Israel, he'd say, 'Why are they sending letters? We're going to get into trouble. They're going to think I'm a spy.'"

Both Hiba and Amgad admit that they have become somewhat estranged from their communities. But they do not seem to mind; more important, they contend that they now want to change the people around them—and feel qualified to do so. "At first I was hopeless. How can I convince those people to forget their pain?" asked Hiba. She decided to invite an Israeli she had met at camp to their home. "My family said it was okay, but for my friends and other people around me, it was, you know, crazy. At first, they didn't believe me. 'What are you saying, an Israeli girl to your home?'" She came a few days later. When Hiba's mother told them that a Palestinian boy had been shot that afternoon near their home, she was surprised at the reaction of her daughter's Israeli friend. Hiba said her mother expected the Israeli girl to be pleased. Instead, "she was very sad and said how bad it was, why did they do that?" said Hiba. "My mother didn't expect an Israeli girl to say that in our house. So she liked her a lot and asked me to invite her again to our house."

At school, Hiba did not try to disguise her new feelings. "Look, I'm thinking in another way," she told her friends, arguing that it was "higher" than their way of thinking because she wanted to talk about the intricacies of the peace process. "I felt I'm supposed to talk with other people. I have many friends now that are older than me: twenty years old, twenty-five, thirty. Really. You can't talk with friends about those things. They don't understand them."

Amgad also said he felt "more elevated" than the "narrow minds" who surrounded him. "I look at people and see how trivial their lives are because they're so ignorant about these things. Everyone has an opinion. They all believe their opinion is right. But how can you have an opinion about some-thing when you don't know it? Now my point of view," he said, "its roots aren't roots of ignorance but roots of knowledge. That's the way I keep my faith, my beliefs, my ideas and opinions about Seeds of Peace and about peace with Israel," he explains. "I always keep reminding myself that my knowledge stems from experience and the others' doesn't."

But a little knowledge can be a dangerous thing. Hiba's teacher was lecturing about Palestinian history, recalled Hiba. "I want to say some-thing!" she said, jumping up. "I was sure she was saying wrong things." Hiba's teacher wasn't pleased. "Please, Hiba, you are the only one who knows about these things, so don't talk," she told her. "But you are saying wrong things," Hiba replied. She explained, "I don't like to see people who are making mistakes. So now it's a problem because now I think that the way I think is higher than the way my teacher thinks."

And Hiba seems prepared to act on that new self-confidence. Several weeks later, on the same day of the interview in her Bethlehem home, she said she had another argument with her teacher. "Do you know what the Israelis think?" Hiba had interrupted. "That's not our lesson today," replied her teacher. "Just let me explain something, what they think," said Hiba. "They think many different things. They have their own history and we have our own history. We must respect their history. Even if I think there is something wrong in their history, I must keep silent. I'm sure that they think that our history is wrong. But they must also respect. That's what you have to do," she implored. "You have to understand the thing you are talking about from all sides, from our side and from their side. I've met Israelis and Palestinians who aren't what the propaganda, what the media says they are or what my . . . the people around me say they are. The thing I've learned," she says, "is that I can maintain my beliefs and know something better."

Omar, a Moroccan, also encountered opposition. "Today I fought with my Arabic teacher," he wrote us. "We were studying a text about wars, and she asked, 'Who must we tell to stop the war?' and then she answered herself, 'The Jews and Netanyahu.'" Omar said that he shot his hand up and asked his teacher, "Have you ever met, and worked with, and slept in the same room with Jews? Have you ever had Jewish friends?" The teacher replied that was impossible because "they are the enemy." Omar said that inflamed him even more. "I told her that, like us, they are sons of Abraham, and I told her about my wonderful experience in Seeds of Peace." She replied that everyone was free to believe whatever they want. "I said, 'Nobody is free to say bad things about people they don't know.'" Omar added that despite the fact that his teacher and many other Moroccans don't like Jews, "I know Seeds of Peace will make peace. I believe it strongly."

Spreading the Word

Many of the youngsters do not cave in to their environments back home. Instead, like a thousand little Atlases, each shouldering the weight of his or her neighborhoods and schools, the youngsters push their friends and schoolmates the way they were pushed at camp. In this way, the program begins to change not a thousand youngsters, but a thousand communities. And the more hostile the people, the harder our graduates seem to work to change them.

"I start step by step," says Abdelsalam, who lives in Nablus, a West Bank town of intense anti-Israeli sentiment. In school, his class was asked to imagine that in fifty or a hundred years Palestine would have an army with advanced weapons and technology. If you were the president of Palestine, and had the power to do anything to the Israelis, what would you do? Every one of them first said they would kill them, drive them out of Palestine, "do what Hitler did to them," he recalled. Someone who knew he had been at Seeds of Peace asked Abdelsalam for his opinion. "Okay, I hate Israelis like you do," he said. "But I can't kill the kids. I can't kill the women or the old men. What can I do? Okay, I'll kill the people who are responsible for my suffering," he said. They took a minute to think about that and then said, "Okay, we'll kill those who are responsible for our suffering." Then Abdelsalam said, "But you know, not all of them are responsible for our suffering. Maybe some of them are forced to do that. Maybe some of the soldiers don't like to do that. But this is their job. So what can they do?" Many students then said, "Okay, we can kill one or two, that's okay. We'll kill the prime minister and another one."

By now, two of his friends were very angry. One of them said, "No. I will kill all of them. I will kill all of them." Abdelsalam said his friend was "very huge," the tallest one in the class. Abdelsalam walked toward him and, standing right next to him, said, "Okay, but if you will kill Shani, I will kill you." Shani is one of Abdelsalam's Israeli friends. "He knows who Shani is so he told me, 'Okay, you can take Shani when there is a war and put her in your house.'" Abdelsalam then asked, "What about Shani's mother? Shani's father? Her friends? What about Shani's dog?" "Okay," his friend blurted out, "I will not kill any of the Israelis. Go away!" Abdelsalam said he was pleased that he was able to persuade his friend to change his mind even if it was "only for a second." He will now wonder why he changed his mind and realize that he did "because there is some right in that—not to kill all of them or not to kill any one of them," said Abdelsalam.

He said he still cannot talk to his grandmother about Seeds of Peace because she was forced to flee her home in Haifa in 1948 and lost her son in the 1967 war. "They are animals—that's what she will tell me," he said. Abdelsalam spends lot of time reading about the conflict. "With my money I bought books, big books, and I read every day and every night." Although concerned that his son might be neglecting his math and science home-work, Abdelsalam's father supports him and says it is good to read "instead of playing football." However, there is resistance. When Abdelsalam wanted to bring Israelis to visit his high school, the Ministry of Education refused permission. So he created a club called "Palestine in Peace" and approached ministry officials with a plan to educate children at nearby schools by pro-viding them with textbooks that are more balanced in their approach. He also has become a facilitator. He introduced Ned Lazarus, who heads our Jerusalem office, to Sami, a Palestinian cousin whose brother was one of five suicide attackers who planted a bomb on Tel Aviv's crowded Ben Yehuda Street. "You see, this cousin, he's a terrorist, as the world says, and Ned is Jewish, our enemy." But he never told Ned about Sami's family. Nor did he tell Ned that he was the first Jew Sami had ever met. "They have met two or three times," said Abdelsalam. "If they knew beforehand that Ned is Jewish and my cousin is a terrorist, they would not talk to each other. But they shake hands and they kiss each other. There is no border between them because they are humans. Now every one of my friends knows about Seeds of Peace and about Ned. They even send him a card on his birthday."

After all, Abdelsalam doesn't blame his old friends. "Before I went to camp, I thought that the Israelis know that they are occupiers," he said. "I didn't know that they think they have the right [to be there], that this is the 'land of dreams' for them and stuff like that. Now in my mind I know that there are two histories, two facts, and one land. Two people and just one land. If there were another land, the problem would be solved. Two facts and two people and just one land. That's the problem."

Before she went to Seeds of Peace, said Bushra, who lives in a refugee camp in Hebron, she felt the same way. "My idea about Israelis is just that they are soldiers, without any people. I didn't think that there are families with children and relatives, just soldiers with a gun, with a weapon. And I thought that all the Israelis, all of them hate Palestinians." She said she learned to make useful distinctions at camp. "There are Israelis who support peace, who agree with the Palestinians, who sympathize with us," she said. That was a revelation to her. It allowed Bushra to open up to Israelis. "I learned some of their traditions, that on Friday they say 'Shabbat Shalom,' that they pray—well, it is not the same as us, but they pray. And they believe in God. And we believe in God. So we have some links." After the July 1997 bombing in the Jerusalem marketplace, she recalled, "we just sat there and we were crying, weeping. We remembered that we are killing each other, the Israelis and the Palestinians, killing each other."

The Olive Branch, the Seeds of Peace newspaper

THE OLIVE BRANCH

Youth Newspaper of the Middle East/A Seeds of Peace Production

Volume 3, Number 3   Spring 1999

ScreenPeace

Seven teenagers are the creators of *Peace of Mind*: The first full-length documentary film produced by Israeli and Palestinian teenagers together

By Ned Lazarus (Washington, D.C.)

Peace of Mind, A message to the world from the youth of the Middle East: (from left to right) Amer Kamal, Reut Elkouby, Yaron Avni, Hazem Zanoun, Yossi Zilberman, Sivan Ranon, Bushra Jawabri, and producer Mark Landsman.

Witnesses to War

Under Attack in Kosovo and Belgrade

Escaping Ethnic Cleansing
by Kreshnik Bajktari (Pristina)

Belgrade Bombed: A Diary
by Tatjana Stetin (Belgrade)

Inside This Issue...

A Young Kosovar's story: Kreshnik Bajktari, an Albanian Kosovar who escaped ethnic cleansing and found temporary refuge in Kibbutz Maagan Michael, is this issue's OLIVE BRANCH INTERVIEW.   *Page 3*

Crossing Borders: Courageous teens explore the culture on "the other side" of the river, the "Green Line" and the Mediterranean... *Pages 4 & 5*

What's On Your Mind?: Serbian, American, Palestinian, Jordanian and Israeli teenagers discuss the ongoing crisis in Kosovo.   *Page 6*

Coexistence Hotline: Tatjana Stetin, a teenager living in Belgrade, describes life under bombardment to THE OLIVE BRANCH.   *Page 7*

THE OLIVE BRANCH Survey: Israeli, Palestinian, Jordanian and Egyptian youth voice their opinion about the recent Israeli election   *Page 8*

Plus letters and the art of Or Keshet...

She too is beginning to impact her friends and family. "My sister and my brother, they ask me, 'Where is *The Olive Branch* [the Seeds of Peace newspaper]? We want to read it.'" Bushra provides fifty copies to her relatives, friends, and teachers in the refugee camp. "Sometimes my little brother, he's in the sixth grade and doesn't know a lot of English, he looks at the picture and says, 'Is she an Israeli?' And I translate in Arabic and he says, as if it is a major discovery, 'Yes, yes, yes . . . they play sports.'" Bushra and her family have welcomed Noa, her best Israeli friend, to their modest home. On the second trip, Noa came with her mother. They brought gifts, exchanged small talk, and walked down the dingy streets of the camp, studiously avoiding any talk of politics. Bushra has visited the homes of Noa, Reut, and Sivan in Israel. "Seeds of Peace strengthened my personality," she says. Bushra rarely watched the news or read newspapers before she went to camp. "Now I am more political. I like to discuss politics with Palestinians and Israelis."

Speaking Up for Peace

Some of the youngsters find themselves stronger because they are able to first test the different waters of their opinions and discover "truths" that reaffirm their earlier beliefs.

At camp, "I became more right wing," said Iddo, even though both he and his family are ardent supporters of Meretz, the left wing of the Israeli Labor Party. In his coexistence workshop, he explained, the Palestinians accused all Israeli settlers of being "terrorists" and demanded that their settlements be demolished. "I had to defend them," he said. An Egyptian in his workshop always brought up Netanyahu. "He said that until Netanyahu is gone, we won't have peace. Personally I agree with him but I couldn't say that because I'm an Israeli. I couldn't say something against my own people. I had to choose between being a radical left-wing Israeli and being an Israeli and I chose the Israeli part."

And yet when he returned, Iddo found life to be somewhat different. Before, he explained, he never paid attention to the crowds at soccer games that yelled "Death to the Arabs" and "Mohammed [the Prophet] is a homosexual." Now when Iddo goes to the games, "I feel like 'Why don't you stand up and say something?' and then I remind myself that there are thirty thousand people in this stadium. Do you really want to stand up and say, 'Arabs are not homosexuals'? Everyone will beat me up. But it makes me feel guilty that I don't do something."

Iddo said that as soon as their flight landed in Tel Aviv, "it was pretty awkward because we talked (on the plane) about how peace is so wonderful.

But when you come back to Israel, peace stops right there, in Ben Gurion Airport. After that, you're a Palestinian and I am an Israeli. I can go anywhere I like, I can leave home anytime but you can't go home whenever you want and you can't leave your home whenever you want. It's frustrating to see how peace stops right here as soon as you give your passport to whoever is checking them." Iddo said he feels a new responsibility toward the Palestinians because "when we were playing basketball and soccer in the street, they were throwing stones at soldiers and hiding in their houses with fear that someone might shoot them. I learned that they suffered the most during the intifada and if I can do something to make them feel better about it, I think it's my duty as an Israeli."

Roy, an Israeli camper, also discovered that "serious things are going on there [in Gaza and the West Bank]—that Palestinians are not treated as human beings." He had been led to believe that all Palestinians support Hamas, "that they all want war. But when I got to speak with them I found out they're not all in one direction like they're blindfolded and when the leader decides something they all have to follow. They don't only do what their government wants them to do. They have their own opinions. It's like they have mouths and ears and eyes and everything."

It is noteworthy that Roy did not make this discovery in his coexistence workshop but in his bunk, where, he said, "it's more personal, more intimate." There he developed a friendship with Mohammed, the Palestinian whose pregnant aunt died because the ambulance taking her to a hospital was prohibited from crossing a Gaza checkpoint. To Roy, it meant a lot that Mohammed took out the clothes he had bought for his parents and eight brothers and sisters and showed them to him. "It was awesome because we really got to speak and we really bonded. We switched T-shirts," Roy said proudly. Mohammed always spoke about his gun wounds, he said, "like his bullet wounds here on the ankle and on the back. Up until then I thought it's a fake. Like I thought it was probably a couple of pricks, not something serious. Then he told me how it hurt him personally and it offended him as a person, not only physically," said Roy.

This exchange, in the confines of their bunk, allowed Roy to see Mohammed not simply as a Palestinian but as a friend. "The first reason that we need to promote peace is not only for us but for them, for the way they live," he said. "They live in awful conditions. For them to go to the cinema, they have to go all the way to Jerusalem, which is not under their control. So they need to get visas and go through the checkpoints and everything—just to see a movie. For me, you know, it's just going to the mall." But what brought it home to Roy was watching Israeli television footage of a Palestinian being shot in the head with rubber bullets. "They showed it fully, no censorship. I saw how ugly and how hateful that rubber bullet can be. And when we speak about metal, it's even worse. So that was the first time I saw what my friends might be facing, you know, in the Gaza Strip. How can I not care how Sa'ad lives or how Amer lives because I care for them. So I cannot just ignore it," he said.

But he is bothered by the attitude of his friends in ways that he says never would have dawned on him before Seeds of Peace. A few days after he returned home in 1997, the bombing took place on Ben Yehuda Street. The next day, shortly after the funerals had been held for the Israelis killed in the attack, Roy and his friends were asked to put up Boy Scout posters. A passerby asked them what they were doing. "Aren't you ashamed to do something like that on a day like today?" he asked. "We have no choice. The Scout ceremony is the day after tomorrow," Roy told him. "Why aren't you putting up posters that say 'Kill the Arabs!'?" asked the passerby. One of Roy's friends replied: "The Scouts is not a political movement. We can't do that in the name of the Scouts." The response upset Roy. It still does. "That's like the stupidest answer I've ever heard," he said, "because when the man says why don't you put up posters that say 'Kill the Arabs!' it's like plastering posters against my friends, against Hassan and Mohammed and Amer." Most Israelis do not see the Palestinians as individuals, he explained. "They don't care about the Palestinians. They just don't want to be shot." That's what the peace process is for them. "For me," said Roy, "it's 'I care about the Palestinians' and I don't want to be shot. I don't want the Palestinians to be shot and I don't want to get hurt. So both sides will be secure. That's what peace is to me."

So Roy, who is fourteen years old, now speaks up in class and has earned the respect of his fellow classmates in Ashdod. "When we get into political conversations, when I speak, everybody shuts up. You know, 'Roy's talking. Let's hear him.' I think people think that I know more than I do, and I've been there and I've seen them, you know, the 'freaks' on the other side."

Amer, a Palestinian, said that one of his friends ridiculed him in front of his entire class. He said that Palestinians and Israelis will go on hating each other forever: "They killed my uncle. . . . How could we live with them?" Amer asked his friend, "Have you ever met an Israeli? Have you ever talked to an Israeli?" His friend said no. "That's the problem. The media," he explained. "They put on the religious Israelis, the ones who want to destroy the Dome of the Rock [the al-Aqsa mosque in Arab East Jerusalem], who want to kill Palestinians, and who want all of Palestine. The same with the Israelis," he said. "They always see Hamas. So they will hate the other side. I told him, you have to know the others." His friend replied, "Okay, you're a Jew. I won't talk with you." But Amer continues to talk with his friends and family about his experiences.

And often the more the students are attacked, the more vocal they become for their new beliefs.

The families of Ibrahim and Sara were publicly attacked at the Friday prayer service in their mosques in Nablus and Hebron. The imam (Muslim prayer leader) called them "traitors" for sending their children to make peace with Israelis, declaring that they should stay and fight and "not talk to" Israelis. Sara's father refused to be intimidated. He got up at 2 A.M. so they would have plenty of time to get through the Israeli checkpoints and to Ben Gurion Airport for the early afternoon flight. Ibrahim said what angered him was the imam's charge that "we went there [to Seeds of Peace] to betray our people." In an unusual act of bravery, he wrote an article for the Arabic newspaper *al-Quds* (the Arabic name for Jerusalem) directly responding to his imam. "I wrote that Israelis aren't as we see them every day, holding guns and all that stuff. They're people—they're human beings who are hoping like us, dreaming like us to have peace in the whole region." Ibrahim wrote, he said, "how we communicated and lived with each other for these twenty-two days so people here would know how things were going on."

But the sharpest attack occurred on the editorial pages of *al-Ahram*, Egypt's leading daily newspaper, where a noted columnist accused the Egyptian delegation of having been brainwashed into betraying the Palestinian cause. Mohammed, an Egyptian, replied in a letter to the editor:

> I would not have replied unless I had been there and checked the camp out myself. I wish you had been there to see how the Israelis and Palestinians came together in a state of coexistence that no one could have imagined. You should not direct your fire against this camp unless you have seen it for yourself. It is NOT brainwashing, sir, as we cannot be more Palestinian than the Palestinians themselves! I would also like to inform you that I am not paid to write to you but am inspired by the lofty spirit I experienced in camp. I'll be glad to explain everything in full to you in case you need more information. By the way, the camp is self-funded and peace lovers donate what they can for it. Their Majesties King Hussein and Queen Noor are but two examples of the greatness of those who support it.

Facing difficulty himself, a Jordanian camper wrote this e-mail to Seeds of Peace:

> The camp made me see the world in a different view. It made me realize something I never did. This thing is that the Israelis are people just like us who deserve to live also in peace, but these few words are really hard to say in front of people, yet I do so, and I try to tell people about my experience.
>
> What hurts me most of all is that some of my closest friends are calling me things such as 'you traitor . . .' just because I stand against them in some points when they talk about Palestine and the peace. . . . You know there is something about Seeds of Peace that makes me proud to be a part of it, no matter what people say . . . and this something was what made me give a lecture to my class about Seeds of Peace [SOP]. It went on so well and after I did it, two girls came to me and I sat with them in our free time and I talked to them about every detail of it. . . .
>
> And then two days ago, when the bombing had occurred, I had a gathering with a group of friends that worked with me in making a camp here in Jordan possible . . . and there in our gathering I sat with almost seven of them and talked to them about camp and what we did there at SOP; you would be shocked to know that four of them were so into it that they wanted to apply for next year.
>
> Last week I had dinner with my parents, and as you know all the people there are older people, friends of my parents and so on. . . . They started to ask me about my summer and what I did, so I started giving them a surface scan of camp, thinking that they won't be interested so much, but it was so astonishing to me to find out that for almost one hour there was no one else talking in the room other than me, and they were all listening and asking questions. . . . It was great.
>
> One last thing—today Sa'ad, Rami, and Lana came over to my house and we worked on some stuff that we will be telling you about soon. . . . One of the things is arranging a trip for the Israeli delegation to visit Jordan. No one must know about this, not even you for now, but I trust you won't tell anyone yet!
>
> Love always,
> Najib

Staying in Touch and Working Together

The very difficulty of the region forces the youngsters to stay in touch with one another and to work to change the communities around them. And as they battle with this, the impact Seeds of Peace has on both the campers and the region grows. Each new graduate has the potential to infect a new community with the spirit of peace.

Sometimes the youngsters seek not only to change their friends and families but also to influence their nation's leaders. Following the violence that occurred in September 1996, after the Netanyahu government opened an archaeological tunnel exiting near the al-Aqsa mosque, a group of Seeds of Peace alumni wanted to go beyond sending messages of condolence to the families of the Palestinians who were shot in the rioting. Motivated by the announcement that Netanyahu and Arafat had been summoned to an emergency summit at the White House, a core group of former campers worked into the night to merge Israeli, Palestinian, Jordanian, and Egyptian reactions into a common text. The effort required intense negotiation as former campers exchanged position statements and argued over what should and should not be included. After many hours of debate on the Internet, the statement was sent to the Seeds of Peace office, which forwarded it to a senior National Security Council official in Washington. The declaration implored the leaders "to reach a compromise. A fast solution to save us from potential disaster. We support you and we are behind you on every step of this long and hard path. Be strong and brave for all of us, for only the brave can make real peace." It was later learned that at the start of the second day of the summit, President Clinton read the message to the Israeli and Palestinian leaders and their delegations.

The candid and forthright tone of teenagers stands in sharp contrast to the muddled nuances of diplomatic dispatches. After another setback in the peace process, the alumni again went into action. Six Egyptian, Israeli, Jordanian, and Palestinian Seeds wrote a letter to Netanyahu and Arafat that they read aloud to Secretary of State Madeleine Albright, the guest of honor at the annual Seeds of Peace dinner in New York in 1998. They asked that Albright, who was about to leave for a meeting with the Israeli and Palestinian leaders in London, deliver the message to them. It read:

> In our history books, the Middle East always appears as the magnificent cross-roads between the three continents of Africa, Asia, and Europe. Yet in reality, for us, the Middle East is merely a battlefield full of hatred, bloodshed, and regret. Unfortunately, we have not tasted its grandness for we are blinded by destructive wars. At Seeds of Peace, we first recognized the significance of peace. And only then did we learn that making peace is much harder than making war. We all realize that the peace process is stalled. It was initiated but the job is not completed. We understand that you both face opposition for launching the peace process, yet those who oppose you do not know what it is like to have peace. All they know is the hatred and prejudice that their society has imposed on them throughout their lives. We at Seeds of Peace had a taste of what it is like to co-exist peacefully. . . . We are writing this letter as people

who have experienced peace temporarily and enjoyed the taste. But we want the whole pie. This is up to you. It is up to you to shape and build our future. Your actions will either make us fight against you to achieve our own peaceful life, or fight with you to build a brighter future for us and for generations to come. In simple . . . MAKE IT WORK!

Albright delivered the letter to the two leaders. But she also asked Noa to write her own personal note to Arafat on the back of her place card, and Kheerallah to do the same to Netanyahu. When she began her meeting with them, these notes were the first thing Albright read to the leaders.

The hope generated by these young people is an indispensable tonic for a world that often seems to have lost hope. When a devastating flood hit Jericho in the spring of 1998, washing away dozens of homes, Sa'eb Erakat, the chief Palestinian negotiator whose daughter attended camp in 1997, said he had not received a single telephone call from any of the Israeli officials with whom he had been negotiating for five years—since the beginning of the Oslo peace process. "But twenty-one Israeli kids, thirteen to fifteen years old, called Dalal to see if she was okay, to see if we were okay," said Erakat. "This is the future. This is what I am working to build, the culture of peace. It's why I am in politics," he added.

Creating New Challenges

As the youngsters become more open to each other, they develop capacities that enlarge the range of possibilities in the Middle East. In May 1998, Seeds of Peace organized a summit to test those new capacities. The Middle East Youth Summit in Villars, Switzerland, brought together seventy-five Israeli, Palestinian, Jordanian, Egyptian, and American alumni for a week of debate and negotiation over the key issues in the peace process, including final status issues such as security, borders, statehood, the refugees' right to return, and Jerusalem. Could a group of Arab and Israeli teenagers do something their leaders had been unable to do? Could they achieve something their leaders were unwilling to even discuss: write a final Israeli-Palestinian peace treaty?

This was an entirely new challenge for the program. In its first five years, Seeds of Peace focused wholly on teaching the participants how to listen to one another and how to find some means of establishing friendships based on shared values, ideas, and interests. What remained to be seen was whether the trust and friendships established at camp—and continued at home—would make a difference when it came to dealing with the difficult, emotionally charged issues that divide the leaders of the region. With this in mind, Seeds of Peace convened the one-week summit.

Its goal was to draft a document that would come up with compromises on all the core issues, paving the way for a final Israeli-Palestinian peace. If the alumni could write such a treaty, they would send a powerful message to their leaders and to their communities: If these teenagers could find ways to resolve their differences, why couldn't the leaders themselves?

After the initial reunion and rekindling of friendships, attention turned to the challenge at hand. There were six committees of twelve, with an equal distribution of national representatives assigned to each. Seeds of Peace divided the groups and carefully assigned the delegates to committees; for example, all of the Israeli and Palestinian delegates on the Jerusalem committee lived in Jerusalem. Two facilitators who had worked with the youngsters at camp were assigned to each committee.

Hardly had the groups begun their deliberations before a crisis erupted, reminiscent of the ones we had confronted at camp in the aftermath of a terrorist attack. Then, as now, the national delegations united together and formed blocs against one another. This new crisis threatened the survival of the entire summit and seemed, like the chanting of the Jerusalem song at camp, to flow from a routine formality, an innocuous oversight that easily could have been avoided. The teenagers had each been given green Seeds of Peace polo shirts to wear during the conference. On the pocket of each shirt a patch had been ironed on with their nation's flag, and underneath was the name, or abbreviation of the name, of their country (e.g., Israel, Egypt, Jordan, USA). Under the Palestinian flag the letters "PNA" appeared, denoting the Palestinian National Authority, the internationally recognized acronym for the freely elected government that represented the Palestinian people. Seeds of Peace followed the official State Department protocol: there was no state of Palestine, at least not yet; the initials PNA identified the group that governed Palestinian territory. The same acronym was used by Palestinian officials to identify themselves at international conferences throughout the world.

This, however, was a source of resentment among the Palestinian delegates to the youth summit. They objected that everyone else had a country and they had theirs. It was called Palestine. They wanted to remove the patch altogether and demanded that other delegations follow suit. Naturally, this was opposed by the Israeli delegation, and members of other delegations also were disinclined to do so. This led to heated debate among the participants, making negotiation over the core issues impossible and threatening the entire conference. Their adult escorts, of course, did exactly what they do at camp. They encouraged their delegations to take a hard line against the "enemy."

Two delegates, however, an Israeli and a Palestinian, began to broker an agreement. They were Ron and Laith, the same Palestinian who played such an instrumental role in resolving the dispute over the Holocaust. Each had the reputation of being uncompromising, a hard-liner in his own group. The others recognized them as the de facto "leaders" of their delegations; everyone knew that if they could work something out, everyone else would go along. While tempers flared, and all substantive work came to a halt, Laith and Ron met secretly in their hotel rooms. It took them almost thirty-six hours, but they did manage a compromise, and an ingenious one at that. Everyone would continue to display their flags on their shirts. But all delegations would be asked to safety pin their nametags just below their patches so that the top of the plastic tags cloaked the words below the flags. Although a full day and a half had been lost, this proved a major breakthrough and within an hour the conference was back on track, with committee meetings extending throughout the night and informal discussions often lasting until morning light. A new hopefulness pervaded the sessions; if they could work through this thorny issue, then surely these youngsters could find a way to settle other disputes.

Each day brought new challenges, new issues, and more laughter and tears. But as the momentum increased toward the last day of the summit, when each committee would be asked to report its conclusions and submit them for a plenary vote, the delegates worked harder and harder to accommodate each other's concerns and "red lines." When, on the last day, each committee reported its conclusions, and the full plenary voted, there was both joy and a sense of true accomplishment, a feeling that something historic had been achieved. Of the six committee reports, four were adopted by a majority that included two-thirds of both the Israelis and the Palestinians; two were adopted by a majority of all Arabs and Israelis but failed to win two-thirds approval.

Among the four reports adopted almost unanimously was the one that addressed the most daunting issue of all, Jerusalem. The committee proposed a solution under which Israel would cede sovereignty over parts of East Jerusalem so that it could become the capital of a Palestinian state but only after an interim period in which there would have to be no terrorism or threats of violence. Both sides gave something up and received something in return. Israel was allowed to run the clock provided it agreed to recognize parts of East Jerusalem as the Palestinian capital when the five-year interim period was over. At that point the Palestinians would recognize West Jerusalem as the eternal capital of Israel. At the heart of the compromise was the recognition of both Israelis and Palestinians that a genuine interim period was needed to help build trust and confidence on both sides. During this period, however, they agreed that the other elements of the final settlement (e.g., the agreement on refugees, settlements, and borders) should be implemented so that their implementation would help transform the climate between the two peoples. What mattered was not whether this compromise or others could be implemented in today's contentious climate, but that they had persevered against enormous odds and achieved something their leaders could not. This happened because they were Seeds of Peace, because they could trust and understand one another, and because they cared for one another as people. Because of all that, and their refusal to quit, these teenagers were able to draft the "Charter of Villars"—a detailed, fifty-page road map for a final Israeli-Palestinian settlement. The entire text of the treaty is available on the Seeds of Peace website, www.seedsofpeace.org.

What made the delegates to this conference different from delegates to other conferences? Why were the negotiations ultimately successful? Certainly the delegates took the issues seriously, as for many of them discussion revolved around their own lives. Negotiation in the Land Committee, for example, revolved around an Arab village and an Israeli settlement. Representatives of both communities were on the committee. Going through the camp experience with one another, establishing trust and a relationship among themselves, and learning how to listen and to understand the other side facilitated the process of negotiation. But this did not guarantee agreement. What did play a critical role in the success of the summit was that the delegates were friends. They understood that despite their differences, which were real and deep, they also had a lot in common. They knew that what they had discovered about one another, and what they shared with one another, made it worth their while to take some risks. If they succeeded, they would all gain even though they might not have all or even a lot of what they had originally wanted.

This knowledge, this wisdom, made the negotiations quite different from those usually conducted by governments or hardened negotiators. The personal relationship that existed between the Israelis and the Palestinians at the negotiating table allowed the discussion to move beyond politics or posturing for position and into the real lives of these negotiators. Thus, agreement over where a line would be drawn marking Israeli territory had real, everyday implications for Ruba, a Palestinian, and her family, who live in an Arab village outside of Jerusalem. Her friend and

Introductory Letter to the Treaty of Villars
May 7, 1998

Dear Leaders,

To all of us, peace represents the hopes and dreams that have always been absent from our lives. The void left by the lack of these realized dreams has forced people to turn to violence as an answer to their problems. For the first time, the Permanent Status negotiations have been started, not by our governments, but by those the peace truly affects. We here at Seeds of Peace have decided that we will make our peace over the negotiations table not over the battlefield. Our leaders have shown us the way, the way of Menachem Begin and Anwar El Sadat and all of those who have sat at the negotiating table since. It is time to forge ahead and not allow the wheel to turn back because our peace is hanging on a very thin rope.

Our goal at this conference was to build a base for the peace we have always wished for. The treaty that is enclosed within might seem like an illusion to those who do not know and understand what we have experienced at Seeds of Peace. Let us assure you that what you are about to read is in fact representative of our beliefs. It was reached behind closed doors and it reflects our desired reality.

We hope that this treaty will act as a model for you, the leaders of our countries, to base your own agreements on or take suggestions from, but at the very least, we are convinced that it will show you that peace between our two nations is possible. We stressed the idea of our common future together because it is the truth, and we hope that this achievement of peace will act as a key into people's minds, opening their thinking to include the benefits of peace.

Seeds of Peace and Novartis have helped make this Middle Eastern Youth Conference possible, and we thank them for having helped us learn so many important lessons. We have realized the difficulty and challenge involved in the negotiation of complex and emotional issues such as the ones we discussed. But we have also realized that when you let people say what they want and what they need, you understand them better, and from understanding you can build respect. Most important of all, we have realized that no matter how complicated an issue may be, we can not turn away in submission. Instead, we must welcome the challenge of shaping our own common future. We felt the responsibility of having to come here, and we did our job. Now it is your turn.

Sincerely,
Israeli, Palestinian, Egyptian, Jordanian and USA Delegates

fellow negotiator, Dana from Israel, knew this about Ruba and could intimately understand her friend's concerns about where the borders would be drawn.

At the summit, as at camp, a crisis was again needed to "push" the delegates to another level. In a sense, they could not have begun the negotiations in earnest without having had some issue arise first. Why has this pattern emerged? Perhaps the participants of the camp or summit are so eager to make friends and/or to make peace that they do so without fully considering the implications. A crisis may be needed to test the friendship and force the campers/delegates to reconsider what they have worked to establish. Perhaps they need to confront the reality of the crisis to understand what is really required of them. The crisis, then, becomes an antidote to the "utopia" of the camp or summit.

Of course, the crisis, if generated internally, such as that which occurred on Culture Night (as opposed to a bombing, which is external to camp), can occur only once some basis for trust has been established. A relationship, however tenuous, must exist. Otherwise the participants would not care enough to feel "betrayed" by their Arab or Israeli friends. At the summit, the Israelis felt betrayed by their Palestinian friends because the Israelis wore their flags with pride and thought the Palestinians would understand that. Meanwhile, the Palestinians felt betrayed because their Israeli friends did not seem to understand or share their point of view. When this issue was resolved by Laith and Ron, everyone was reassured that their friends from the other side were indeed worthy of their trust and compassion and were willing to negotiate not just in good faith, but as friends. The connection that held them together held up, and instead of trying to call the negotiations off, the youngsters achieved what their leaders had failed to do.

Alumni

The Strength of Community

In order for our Arab and Israeli alumni to continue to promote the goals of the Seeds of Peace, they need our continued support. To help them stage events, meet one another, and stay in touch on a regular basis, Seeds of Peace maintains a staff in Jerusalem, publishes a newspaper, and has developed an Internet site. In October 1999, we also took a long-term lease on a building in Jerusalem. It is situated on the old border between East and West Jerusalem, on French Hill directly across the street from the dormitories of Hebrew University and less than a quarter of a mile from the large Arab town of Issaweyeh.

The office in Jerusalem is in constant communication with hundreds of graduates. It schedules weekly reunions, exchange visits to high schools and homes, and trips to neighboring countries. The office staff, headed by Ned Lazarus, Falestin Shehadeh, Roy Sharone, and Sami Al-Jundi, has been invaluable, among other things, in helping alumni arrange travel to stay in contact. The office also oversees the publication of *The Olive Branch*, a newspaper written and edited by Arab and Israeli alumni and laid out in the office of a publisher in Ramallah by a team of Israeli and Palestinian graduates. As the resources of the office have grown, the youngsters have been able to extend the scope of their activities. During spring 1998, the first programs to include other youngsters began, including a basketball team made up of Israeli and Palestinian Seeds and their friends from their own communities.

The program has grown quickly on the Internet too. The space the Net provides for "chat rooms" and electronic communication allows the youngsters to cross borders without leaving their homes. This is particularly important in the West Bank and Gaza Strip, where merely visiting a friend in Israel means spending days or weeks to obtain the numerous permits and passes required. Communication on the Internet is virtually instantaneous and generally private; like camp, it fosters dialogue with little supervision and no censorship. Online discussions on Seedsnet range from friendly chatter to in-depth political and personal exchanges. Our Seeds of Peace group e-mail will soon go out to almost a thousand graduates. From the e-mail we have received already, it's clear the youngsters take to the technology as a powerful way of staying in contact and continuing their discussions.

After the youngsters return to the region, the Israeli graduates will sooner or later (and sometimes only a few months later) have to perform their military service. This has always proved to be a difficult and sensitive subject for the Israeli Seeds. Recently Omer, who was about to enter the army, raised the question of what he should do if he is ordered to shoot at a crowd of Palestinians and recognizes one of them as a friend from Seeds of Peace: "This situation is very hard for soldiers like us, who have friends from the other side. The million-dollar question for us is: Should we really fight a war we don't believe in? Would you fight the war, knowing you might harm your friends and their families?" The question provoked many thoughtful suggestions from Israelis and Palestinians alike, though none attempted to tell Omer what to do. Gil, an Israeli, remarked that "each one of us has to decide which responsibility is more important: Your people, or your friend."

"It's the greatest invention on earth," says Roy, an Israeli, about the Internet. "We have this organized chat every week. I have two people who if I don't get to chat or e-mail them every day, I call them to see what's wrong. Like when a bombing occurs, it's really important to me that I can speak online with my friends because that's the time that only they could understand me, people who were there for me in camp. That they can speak with me at that time, that's really important to me—to have this instant connection."

Seeds of Peace initiated a computer and Internet training program in 1998 as an official part of its camp curriculum. It has now become one of our most consistent tools for sustaining the effects of the camp program.

When Moran, an Israeli who had just returned home from camp, found herself accused by her friends of making friends with the enemy and selling out her country, she immediately went to her computer and started writing. The next day responses to Moran started flooding the SeedsNet. (See this page and page 108 for Moran's message and one of the replies she received.) For instance, Shira, who had never met Moran, wrote, "But this is what Seeds is about, I think—getting to know what your real inside is, what your attitude towards 'the other side' is. . . . I think what we changed mostly, was ourselves. Our thinking. Our personal 'Me.' We came home so different, so allegedly 'wiser,' so defensive of our used-to-be-enemies. . . . If you find yourself tough enough, believing enough, Seed enough, fight for it. Strive for your own ideals." Palestinians, Jordanians, and Arab Israelis as well as Jewish Israelis sent their support.

Date: Wed, 02 Sep 1998 13:33:18 PDT

From: Moran from Israel

To: Everyone @ seedsofpeace.org

Subject: it's hard

For the first time in a long long time I'm going to be serious. I need your help. Me and my friends got together two days ago. Everything was going just fine, when they started talking about the army and the state of the country.

I knew the conversation would end bad, and soon they started to speak about Arabs. I defended the Arab side, thinking that I was in for a nice long political discussion. But that didn't happen. What did happen was that my best friend got up and started shouting at me. He said that ever since I got back from camp I've been acting different, that I forgot where I came from and where I've returned to.

From his words: "I don't understand, is this camp really more important than your friends? After all, you have changed nothing. All you did is to make friends with some other kids. That is all good when you're there but here things are different. It's not that simple."

That got me thinking. Did we really make a change? Does anyone outside of Seeds of Peace think as we do? Am I really a bad person for not thinking the same as ALL my friends? It's hard. I felt very much alone. Please reassure me that every thing is just fine.

I love you all and miss you.

—Moran

Date: Thu, 03 Sep 1998 11:02:03 PDT

From: Rosy from Jordan

To: Everyone @ seedsofpeace.org

Subject: to moran . . .

hi everyone, and especially moran

i just want to tell you that you are not the only person that goes through that . . .

at first you might start doubting yourself and thinking that you might have done something wrong

but the more discussions you have, the more convinced you will be of what we are doing in seeds of peace, and no matter what anyone tells you, we have made a difference.

don't listen to what people are trying to tell you. they don't know what we all have been through this summer. i can't say that i blame them for exploding in our faces sometimes and accusing us of forgetting who we were. because they don't know. they haven't had the experience that we have had . . .

finally I just want to tell you that every time that you have a hard time explaining to people your beliefs, try to remember the love that you carry for all of your arab friends and it will all come to place . . .

trust me . . . been there . . . done that . . .

and it works.

speak from your heart and I am sure people will respect what you are saying even if they don't come to fully believe it. and just remember how much we all love you and that we all support you. take care of yourself sweety

and keep that smile going

luv u all

A little later, Moran posted this message:

Dear Seeds,

I would like to thank you all from the depth of my heart for your e-mails and phone calls. You were really there for me. Maybe you'd like to know what happened in the end. Well, I printed out all your replies. Then I met all my friends and asked them what is the most important thing in a friendship? They answered, "be there for one another." Then I gave them all of the letters. After they looked at them they told me: 'We're sorry, we didn't know the depth of what happened over there to all of you, we just couldn't begin to understand, and if what your new friends told you, well, from now on they're friends to us as well.

I can try to express my gratitude, but I won't be any good at it . . .

Love Moran

Conclusions

Changing the World

The story of Moran, an Israeli who found sustenance in the e-mails of her Arab friends; the story of Bushra, a Palestinian who returned to the village of her grandmother to eat Shabbat dinner with the Israeli settler who now lives there; the story of Hiba, who corrects her own teacher's prejudice about Israeli history; the story of Eran, who now says *Palestine* because he understands what it means to a Palestinian—these are the stories of inspiration that we seek to create at Seeds of Peace. They are inspiring because they are real, because these young people have understood that they must take real risks, personal risks, to reap the rewards of lasting friendships. Laith, the Palestinian who asked to visit the Holocaust Museum, has changed his perspective and his politics. Tomer, who realized on the soccer field his own prejudice, now has new friendships with Palestinians and works to keep those friendships alive. Amer and Abdelsalam risk their friendships at home every day as they continue to convince those around them to understand the other side.

These accomplishments are not easily attained. We work hard to create the right conditions: neutrality, an insistence on basic respect, a feeling of safety and support. We work hard to build a community in which the youngsters can take pride. We work hard to implement a schedule that brings them so close together that they are forced to throw out stereotypes and to re-envision their enemy. It begins on the day after they arrive, when each flag is raised and each anthem is sung outside the entrance to our camp. We want each delegation to feel the pride of place, to be intensely proud of their national and cultural heritage. It is that separateness, and their knowledge that we are aware of it and value it, that allows them to leave their individual baggage behind and bond over the course of the ensuing three weeks. Our facilitators work to help the youngsters open up and share their own experiences and feelings. It took Yitzhak Rabin and Yasser Arafat whole lifetimes to acknowledge the need for each other, to begin to reconcile themselves and their nations. Only as old age approached did these men discover the humility, the sense of vulnerability—the need for risk-taking—that peacemaking entails. We are trying to foster this awareness within youngsters thirteen to fifteen years old. Within a community of support, our youngsters find the honesty and forthrightness needed for far-reaching change to occur.

Forced to continually explore their own lives while exposed firsthand to the suffering of their enemies, the youngsters embark on a journey of discovery. Each step is difficult. Making friends with the youngster by your bed means overcoming long-held, physical fears. Speaking candidly with an enemy across the table means discovering regions of hatred and shame that many adults refuse to face. Dropping the urge to negotiate and adopting the vulnerability needed to share their deep-seated beliefs takes courage. The youngsters must overcome a great deal of embarrassment and awkwardness to share their own sense of suffering and pain. We make sure they persist in their efforts to share the experiences that have sculpted their own sense of suffering. When they share these stories, they purge themselves of their self-absorption, thereby relieving the pressure to prove their own righteousness. No longer blind to all but their own suffering, they reengage with each other, this time seeing their own pain reflected in the enemy. They acquire compassion. Reaching out and acknowledging the pain of the other side becomes an act so powerful that it allows the youngsters to finally share their sense of suffering together and look to the future with a common mission. As friends and as neighbors, they search for ways to recreate the vision of peace they experienced at camp. They bring the community they have created in Maine to the Middle East.

Each camp is different, of course. Each has it own unpredictable mixture of personalities and circumstances, its own dynamics, atmosphere, and character. Yet, in each case, our success in fostering a process of change within the youngsters depends upon their learning the same set of fundamental lessons:

■ *They meet "the enemy" as a human being.* The youngsters, no matter how open-minded they might be, are shocked to see—for the first time in their lives—that the enemy is just another teenager. Their fears and suspicions and the "warnings" of their friends back home disappear as they find out how easy it is to live in the same bunk or play on the same team as someone from the "other side."

■ *They become aware that their knowledge of history is biased and incomplete.* The youngsters are amazed to discover that what they have been told about the conflict is only half the story. They learn that each side has overemphasized its strong points and ignored, belittled, or ridiculed what the other side considers important. Armed with new knowledge, our youngsters often go home ready to challenge their teachers and inspired to begin reading books that provide another point of view.

■ *They learn an awareness of the stereotypes and prejudices in each community.* As one youngster put it, "We are not fighting each other; we are fighting the masks of the devil we have painted on each other's faces." They are able to discover by themselves, in the context of a number of structured activities, the massive gap between the perceptions that exist in each community about the "other" and their own experience of meeting the other face to face. In the words of one youngster, "Today is the death of my prejudices."

■ *They learn to distinguish individuals within the notion of the "other side."* Our youngsters come to realize that they can blame very little on the other youngsters around them. Although initially they regard the other side as a homogeneous—and guilty—bloc, most campers learn to distinguish their new friends from those who were responsible for the crimes of the past. Face to face with youngsters who have not done anything to them, the campers begin to challenge policies that could harm their new friends in the future.

■ *They learn that their own stories can have powerful effects on the experiences of other youngsters.* Although at first afraid to share their own experiences, as they open up to one another they discover that what they have to say is important and can have a profound effect on those around them. Many youngsters arrive believing that they can do very little to change the world, yet when they experience the reaction to their own stories, they discover their own power. Seeing people absorb their message also relieves them of the burden to continue focusing on it. As one youngster said, "I feel like now I am an empty vessel."

■ *They learn to understand and acknowledge one another's pain.* The campers generally begin without any understanding of the other side's pain. Understandably, they are immersed in their own. As they listen to the other side's stories of individual and collective suffering, they undergo a transformation; now they begin to understand the cyclical nature of the conflict and the need to end all suffering. In the process they comprehend that the competition over who has suffered most also must end.

■ *They learn that they have power over their own identity.* The youngsters arrive believing that they must represent the policies of their government partly to ensure their status as "real" Israelis or Arabs. Many expect that Seeds of Peace will try to erase their identities, to make them feel less Israeli or Palestinian. Instead they find their hold on their identities to be stronger. They learn that making peace requires a deep understanding of who they are and that peace is only possible if it acknowledges their separate identities.

■ *They learn that being fully honest allows them to express themselves more freely.* Many youngsters come to camp unwilling to express their own emotions or beliefs. When they begin honestly sharing their thoughts, they are able to see the progress that taking such risks creates.

■ *They learn that they are important.* The youngsters learn that opportunities to deliver their own messages and to receive those of the enemy are rare and must be cherished. Saluted by political leaders and the media for their success, they understand that each of them is worthy of sharing their thoughts with the larger community.

■ *They make a conscious decision to be peacemakers.* The youngsters understand that becoming a peacemaker requires a strong personal commitment, one that has specific and practical consequences for them when they return home. Among other things, it means staying in contact with other Seeds across highly restricted borders, remaining outspoken and honest with one's friends, and educating one's parents, peers, and the larger community about the realities of the other side.

■ *They become a community willing to help one another sustain their mission.* They make a personal effort not only to continue their activities but also to support one another in their community of peacemakers. Understanding how difficult being a peacemaker can be, the youngsters readily support each other through difficult times and experiences.

Few people believe that such a community can exist. One of our Israeli graduates noted that "we spend billions of shekels each day preparing for the possibility of war. But we spend nothing preparing for the possibility of peace." His observation is a profound one. We have invested billions of dollars in trying to find a cure for cancer. Have we invested in trying to discover the causes of war and how to treat the symptoms that precede it? Have we made a serious effort to break the cycles of violence before conflicts erupt? Indeed, do we believe that peace is even achievable and sustainable, a goal worth expending resources for? The sad answer is no. Almost a trillion dollars is spent annually on arms purchases throughout the world. The United States alone spent $20 billion on the war in Kosovo. The motives for launching that war may have been laudable, but how much more effectively might that $20 billion—or a small fraction of it—have been used had it been spent on earlier programs to reconcile long-time enemies.

When wars end in the Balkans or the Middle East and peace accords are signed, peacekeeping troops are dispatched to separate the two warring parties. But the peacekeepers are seldom withdrawn on schedule—not least because so few resources are devoted to bringing the two sides together again. It is time to embrace the other half of the peacemaking coin. It is time to spend the resources required to bring people together. It is time to launch a major new initiative worldwide to build peace in the hearts of future generations of leaders.

I have been a journalist for thirty years and have experienced firsthand the cynicism of my former media colleagues toward peacemaking efforts, particularly among children. Yet what better place to start? If Roy can help explain Palestinian suffering in his Israeli classroom, if Kheerallah can convince his friends in East Jerusalem to join a Palestinian-Israeli basketball team, the opportunities for peacemaking are real. They may not be easy: as Laith explained, "making peace is harder than making war; it takes time, it takes care, it takes patience." Peace is something that must be fought for. If we believe that peace is indeed attainable, something worth fighting for, we can transform individuals and institutions. The League of Nations defined countries as entities "capable of waging war." Nations can just as realistically become engines for waging peace. Conflict will never dissolve. We live in a world of limited resources and complicated history, and few areas have as complex a history as the Middle East.

By working with Seeds of Peace, however, the Arab and Israeli governments are already working to create peace. Through publicizing the program in their schools, selecting the participants, and honoring us with high-level visits by senior officials, the governments are sending a message about the importance of peace between ordinary people. But they could do far more. If nations saw themselves as responsible for preparing their people for the peaceful resolution of conflict, they would surely spend less on arms and more on arming themselves for peace. If people saw their leaders as responsible for finding peaceful solutions, leaders would surely make it much less difficult for people to meet openly with the enemy.

We ask our youngsters all the time what peace means to them—they usually use it as an opportunity to advance their cause: "It means security and an end to fear," say the Israelis. "It means an end to the settlements," say the Palestinians. They are both right. But peace at our program is neither a tie-dyed hug-fest, nor just another word to justify one people's righteousness. Peace at camp means honest, unambiguous expression. It means allowing one's experiences to surface so that human connections can be made. It means making the commitment to understand each other and to understand ourselves. Shouq, a Jordanian teenager, said, "You cannot make peace with your enemy until you have gone to war with yourself."

I remember walking into a coexistence session where all fourteen participants were sobbing. They were crying because they valued one another and someone had said something that had hurt them all. The scene appeared hopeless. I thought I was at a funeral. And yet that moment gave me hope. They appeared to be crying for all the victims of the long Arab-Israeli conflict. Indeed, they were not embarrassed to be crying in front of each other. They were unafraid to share one of the most intimate moments of our being as humans. The poison and the blood shed in decades of violence seemed to flow in their tears. Seeds of Peace, in the final analysis, is a detoxification program. It allows the accumulated generations of hatred to pour out. What struck me in that moment was how vulnerable each of these youngsters had become. They were sharing the most noble emotion of all, the courage to appear weak—and human—in front of their enemy. Those tears would become the glue to bind them to a new future, one in which all teenagers, no matter how hard they fought to prevail in their suffering, would begin to care for one another.

At the end of every summer I feel a mixture of sadness and hope, of despair and exhilaration. Many Israelis are still so fearful that they cannot accept it when a Palestinian says he comes from "Palestine." For them, the word is fraught with danger. Many Palestinians also still feel the pain of *al-Nakba* so acutely that they cannot give up the dream of evicting the Jews and returning to their grandparents' homes in Israel. They have just as hard a time telling Israelis that when they say "Palestine," they mean a state that will coexist with Israel—in peace and securtiy.

Our experience at Seeds of Peace has taught me that change is possible. But it has also underscored the chasm that continues to exist between the "peace" made by politicians and the sentiments of the people themselves. Historic compromises reached almost a decade ago by Yasser Arafat and Yitzhak Rabin have yet to be accepted by many Israelis and Palestinians. Treaties are, after all, just pieces of paper. Unless they are translated into reality by changes in the way that textbooks, governments, and the media portray the "other side," peace will remain elusive.

Even with such changes, it will take several generations for populations reared on fear, mistrust, and hatred to begin to trust one another. But I believe we are planting seeds of understanding and hope in the hearts of the most important constituency of all, the next generation of leaders. As an Israeli put it, " The Palestinians said land is more important than life because they grew up without the land. We understood that. We said life is more important than land because we grew up without life, with the risk of losing life. And they understood that." In understanding each other's need for that tradeoff of land for security lies the seeds of mutual recognition and respect. In the end, it is only when one side begins to truly care about the other and for the other's safety and well-being that peace has a chance.

In the summer of 1999, as one of our camps was coming to a close, I was handed a letter by Or, an Israeli youngster. "What does it mean being 'a seed of peace'?" Or's letter began by asking. "What are we planting?"

> These questions I asked myself before I came to the camp, but now I'm proud to say that we are planting a seed of peace, harmony, and friendship, things that you can't touch unless you close your eyes, look into your heart, and say: "I live in harmony with my neighbors." "I made my enemy my friend."
>
> Believing in these things will only make my life better.
>
> At the beginning of this camp I told myself that I was coming to defend my nation's stances and protect its name. But now I know that admitting that the other side is there is not wrong, and as an Israeli I know that being pro-

Palestinian does not make you anti-Israeli—it only makes you stronger and safer.

For each of us, peace is something else. For me, it's only the feeling that there is someone thinking about you there, in the land you call "enemy." What does land matter when we can't all behave and respect everyone as human beings?

I give you my promise to make sure my Arab and Palestinian friends will be safe and will be treated like human beings. We can open the ways to peace.

John Wallach left a distinguished career as the foreign editor of the Hearst Newspapers to found Seeds of Peace. His articles were nationally syndicated by the New York Times News Service and he won numerous awards for uncovering the Iran-Contra affair and for his coverage of the Egyptian-Israeli Camp David Summit. John has appeared frequently on PBS, NBC, CBS, ABC, CNN, BBC, and National Public Radio. His efforts to foster understanding among peoples have won praise from President Mikhail Gorbachev, President Bill Clinton, Prime Minister Yitzhak Rabin, and King Hussein, who presented him with Jordan's Legion of Honor. He is the coauthor, with his wife, Janet, of three books about the Arab-Israeli conflict: *Still Small Voices, The New Palestinians*, and *Arafat: In the Eyes of the Beholder*. Since 1992, John and Janet have been Visiting Fellows of the Woodrow Wilson Center for Scholars, and John recently received an honorary doctorate from Middlebury College. He was a Senior Fellow at the United States Institute of Peace in 1998–99.

Michael Wallach, a 1998 honors graduate of Cornell University, is project director of the Seeds of Peace CD-ROM Program. He was awarded Cornell's Freeman Prize in peace studies and the Innovation in Service award for introducing literacy classes in the New York State prison system and for his work in fostering Arab-Jewish dialogue.

James Lukoski, a freelance photojournalist, has extensively covered the Middle East on assignment for major international magazines. When not on assignment, he teaches at the International Center of Photography in New York City.

United States Institute of Peace

The United States Institute of Peace is an independent, nonpartisan federal institution created by Congress to promote research, education, and training on the peaceful management and resolution of international conflicts. Established in 1984, the Institute meets its congressional mandate through an array of programs, including research grants, fellowships, professional training, education programs from high school through graduate school, conferences and workshops, library services, and publications. The Institute's Board of Directors is appointed by the President of the United States and confirmed by the Senate.

Chairman of the Board: Chester A. Crocker
Vice Chairman: Max M. Kampelman
President: Richard H. Solomon
Executive Vice President: Harriet Hentges

Board of Directors

Chester A. Crocker (Chairman), James R. Schlesinger Professor of Strategic Studies, School of Foreign Service, Georgetown University
Max M. Kampelman, Esq. (Vice Chairman), Fried, Frank, Harris, Shriver and Jacobson, Washington, D.C.
Dennis L. Bark, Senior Fellow, Hoover Institution on War, Revolution and Peace, Stanford University
Theodore M. Hesburgh, President Emeritus, University of Notre Dame
Seymour Martin Lipset, Hazel Professor of Public Policy, George Mason University
W. Scott Thompson, Professor of International Politics, Fletcher School of Law and Diplomacy, Tufts University
Allen Weinstein, President, Center for Democracy, Washington, D.C.
Harriet Zimmerman, Vice President, American Israel Public Affairs Committee, Washington, D.C.

Members ex officio
Phyllis Oakley, Assistant Secretary of State for Intelligence and Research
Daniel H. Simpson, Vice President, National Defense University
Walter B. Slocombe, Under Secretary of Defense for Policy
Richard H. Solomon, President, United States Institute of Peace (nonvoting)

Jennings Randolph Program for International Peace

This book is a fine example of the work produced by senior fellows in the Jennings Randolph fellowship program of the United States Institute of Peace. As part of the statute establishing the Institute, Congress envisioned a program that would appoint "scholars and leaders of peace from the United States and abroad to pursue scholarly inquiry and other appropriate forms of communication on international peace and conflict resolution." The program was named after Senator Jennings Randolph, of West Virginia, whose efforts over four decades helped to establish the Institute.

Since 1987, the Jennings Randolph Program has played a key role in the Institute's efforts to build a national center of research, dialogue, and education on critical problems of conflict and peace. More than a hundred senior fellows from some thirty nations have carried out projects on the sources and nature of violent international conflict and the ways such conflict can be peacefully managed or resolved. Fellows come from a wide variety of academic and other professional backgrounds. They conduct research at the Institute and participate in the Institute's outreach activities to policymakers, the academic community, and the American public.

Each year approximately fifteen senior fellows are in residence at the Institute. Fellowship recipients are selected by the Institute's board of directors in a competitive process. For further information on the program, or to receive an application form, please contact the program staff at (202) 457-1700.

Joseph Klaits
Director

The Enemy Has a Face

Design by Hasten Design Studio, Inc.
Additional layout by Helene Y. Redmond
Photographs by James Lukoski
Maps prepared by Michael Soneson
Proofread by Karen Stough
Edited by Nigel Quinney